THE NIGHTTIME NOVELIST

Finish Your Novel
in Your Spare Time

JOSEPH BATES

WD
WRITER'S DIGEST
BOOKS
WritersDigest.com
Cincinnati, Ohio

The Nighttime Novelist. Copyright © 2010 by Joseph Bates. Manufactured in China. All rights reserved. No other part of this book may be reproduced in any form or by any electronic or mechanical means including information storage and retrieval systems without permission in writing from the publisher, except by a reviewer, who may quote brief passages in a review. Published by Writer's Digest Books, an imprint of F+W Media, Inc., 4700 East Galbraith Road, Cincinnati, Ohio 45236. (800) 289-0963. First edition.

For more resources for writers, visit www.writersdigest.com/books.

To receive a free weekly e-mail newsletter delivering tips and updates about writing and about Writer's Digest products, register directly at http://newsletters.fwpublications.com.

14 13 12 11 10   5 4 3 2 1

Distributed in Canada by Fraser Direct, 100 Armstrong Avenue, Georgetown, Ontario, Canada L7G 5S4, Tel: (905) 877-4411. Distributed in the U.K. and Europe by David & Charles, Brunel House, Newton Abbot, Devon, TQ12 4PU, England, Tel: (+44) 1626-323200, Fax: (+44) 1626-323319, e-mail: postmaster@davidandcharles.co.uk. Distributed in Australia by Capricorn Link, P.O. Box 704, Windsor, NSW 2756 Australia, Tel: (02) 4577-3555.

Library of Congress Cataloging-in-Publication Data
Bates, Joseph, 1972-
The nighttime novelist : finish your novel in your spare time / by Joseph Bates. -- 1st ed.
    p. cm.
Includes index.
ISBN 978-1-58297-846-8 (alk. paper)
1. Fiction--Technique. 2. Fiction--Authorship. I. Title.
PN3365.B333 2010
808.3--dc22   2010012334

media

Edited by: Lauren Mosko Bailey

Designed by: Terri Woesner

Cover illustration by: Andrew Bannecker

Production coordinated by: Mark Griffin

DEDICATION

For Jacob and Emma

ACKNOWLEDGMENTS

My thanks to the fine people at Writer's Digest for making this book possible, including Jane Friedman for the green light, Kelly Nickell for the inspiration and championing, and Lauren Mosko Bailey for helping show me the way (again). My gratitude to the English departments at Clemson University and the University of Cincinnati–in particular Ron Moran, Harold Woodell, Keith Lee Morris, Michael Griffith, Jim Schiff, and especially Brock Clarke–for teaching me what I know, and to my generous colleagues at Miami University of Ohio for the opportunity to pass it on.

Special thanks to my family and friends for their endless encouragement and support. I wouldn't be here without you.

And, in the "for everything" category, my heartfelt thanks to Jessica.

ABOUT THE AUTHOR

Joseph Bates's fiction and nonfiction have appeared in *The South Carolina Review, Identity Theory, Lunch Hour Stories, The Cincinnati Review, Shenandoah, and Novel & Short Story Writer's Market.* He holds a Ph.D. in comparative literature and fiction writing from the University of Cincinnati and currently teaches in the creative writing program at Miami University in Oxford, Ohio. Visit the author online at www.nighttimenovelist.com.

TABLE OF CONTENTS

INTRODUCTION

I'd originally intended to begin this book by listing a number of famous authors who held day jobs and then did their best work by night.

Of course I would've mentioned Franz Kafka, who spent his days at a cramped desk at Workers Accident Insurance Institute of Prague and his nights hunched over his writing desk at home, making stories and novels so fantastic and strange it would be necessary to coin a term, *Kafkaesque*, to describe them.

I might've mentioned William Carlos Williams (practicing physician) or Joseph Heller (advertising) or Toni Morrison (publishing). I could bring up stories, by now well known, of authors currently making more-than-comfortable livings who began by stealing time to write: Stephen King, for example, who taught high school English, or John Grisham, who worked as an attorney, or J.K. Rowling, who, as the story goes, was actually *fired* from her job and was on welfare when she began writing *Harry Potter and the Philosopher's Stone*. For a bit of comic relief, I'd bring up William Faulkner's stint as a postmaster ... comic because I find it difficult to believe any mail was actually delivered.

But as I kept doing research for this introduction, the list kept getting bigger and bigger, as did the names on it. Names so big, in fact, I had trouble picturing these authors doing anything *but* writing: Agatha Christie, Sir Arthur Conan Doyle, Mark Twain, Charles Dickens, Herman Melville, Nathaniel Hawthorne. Admittedly, every writer-friend I know works a day job, so I don't know why I'd be surprised at the number of famous authors who had them, too. I suppose it never occurred to me that my bookshelves might be filled with masterpieces by men and women who put in their hours at a workplace, came home and found a quiet corner, and then wrote. From writers, in other words, whose days might've looked suspiciously like mine. Or like yours.

The truth is, there are only a handful of writers working who make their living solely by their fiction. Most are people who put in long days, have families to care for or responsibilities to meet, work hard to make the bills, could probably use a rest, and who nevertheless feel compelled, after all is said and done, to sit by themselves and write stories. These Nighttime Novelists publish the majority of books on the shelves. Some teach or go to school, some write or edit, some work office jobs, some work construction, but all of them have decided that there's something wonderful, something worthwhile, in staying up late or getting up a little early or spending their weekends working on a novel. It makes them feel like they're part of something bigger than themselves. It feels *meaningful*. I agree with them completely ... and if you're reading this book, I assume you agree, too.

The aim of this book is to help you join those ranks. This is not a plan or a club or a cult; there's no timetable or calendar inside with dates marked for you; there are no dues to pay (at least not to me) and no obligations (at least not to me). The book is not going to demand you write between 9 PM and 1 AM every night and then send me a postcard telling me you did it. In fact, all of you will have slightly different working habits and methods. Some of you might be Early Morning Novelists. Most will be Weekend Novelists. Some may even be Holiday Novelists. You know much better than I when your best time to work is, and this book won't try to dictate that for you. What this book *will* do is help you work better and smarter, help you make the most of your writing time. Your time is valuable, after all ... and you've chosen something very valuable to spend it on.

It's my hope that *The Nighttime Novelist* will help you spend it wisely.

PART ONE
BEGINNINGS

Beginning a novel is always an intimidating, self-conscious exercise, like waving your hand dramatically and saying Let There Be Light. And make no mistake: You are, indeed, creating a brand new world every time you write, one that didn't exist before you said so.

Sometimes you'll be an active and involved creator, stepping in and asserting control over the work where it's needed. But at other times, especially once the fictional world really begins taking on a life of its own, your biggest job will be to try to keep up and record the story as it tells you where it's headed next. Those are great writing days—hours passing by before you've even looked at the clock, your fingers clacking the whole time. You'll get great sleep these nights ... if, that is, the story will let you. But a story can only begin directing you if, first, you've set up the fundamentals of the story in the right ways.

That's what the following lessons and exercises will help you do: craft your opening and build your world line by line, scene by scene, chapter by chapter, until you've hit certain markers and set up a complete, compelling first act. The beginning is important stuff: This is your reader's invitation into your fictional world, and how well you construct the world from the start determines whether the reader will accept the invitation, decide to stay for the next three hundred pages or so, or move on.

Let's start at the very beginning—the initial idea—and make sure we're doing everything we can to grab the reader's attention and keep it.

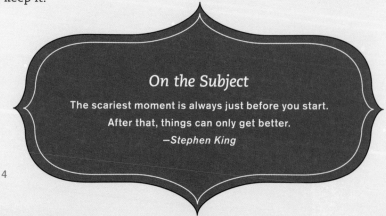

On the Subject

The scariest moment is always just before you start.
After that, things can only get better.
—*Stephen King*

DEVELOPING INITIAL IDEAS

Every novel you've ever read—including that one that felt so real, you were surprised when you closed it to find you were sitting on your couch or propped up in bed—began in the same simple way: with a fleeting thought or image that caught the writer's attention, held it for a moment, and led him to begin asking What if ...?

I don't mean that the writer began debating the idea intellectually, trying to complicate the idea on purpose. Rather, the writer witnessed something everyday that led him to begin daydreaming, not just asking questions but imagining possible answers, constructing scenarios. Writing a novel begins not in a moment of work but a moment of play, with an intriguing idea or image inspiring the mind toward unexpected leaps and unanticipated connections. (Meanwhile the rest of the checkout line behind you is wondering why you aren't moving forward but are instead staring off dreamily into space.)

On the Subject

It struck me with the force of revelation. On the front page of the *Times* there was a headline on the left ... "Giants Capture Pennant" ... and on the right side of the page, symmetrically matched ... "Soviets Explode Atomic Bomb." Something about the juxtaposition of these two events made me think there was something here I wanted to explore. I wasn't sure at the moment quite what.

—*Don DeLillo, on* Underworld

This is something that all of us used to do as kids and that writers, thankfully, never outgrew. And for those of us stealing time to write, the implication should be heartening: Your work doesn't begin the moment you sit down in front of the computer, boring down on the blank screen, wondering what you should write about and trying to "come up" with something. There are story ideas all around us, every day—ideas rich enough to sustain a lifetime of work—if we're willing to pay close attention to those things we glimpse out of the corner of our eye, as John Updike once put it, and then let our imaginations linger.

Of course, not everything we glimpse will be enough to form the basis of a novel. What makes a novel idea sustainable is the degree to which it contains, or at least suggests, all other aspects of the book: character, conflict, plot, tone, theme, more. Put another way, the best ideas already have the potential for a full world. Drawing out that potential, building on it in ways both surprising and inevitable, is the focused work of the novelist.

BUILDING FROM THE IDEA UP

A sustainable novel idea, as we've already said, is one in which all other elements of story seem contained within it, or are at least suggested by it, and build logically one upon the other. This, in fact, is how the mental process works when we encounter these glimpses or early sparks of stories and begin our purposeful daydreaming: The single image leads us to a reaction or thought, which suggests the next idea or thought, which suggests the next. Soon we're at an idea six or seven steps removed from the first but directly related to it in a clear progression we can trace back.

If this all sounds a bit mysterious, there's a reason for that: It is. The creative leaps the subconscious mind makes in those moments of daydreaming are worth a thousand sessions of sitting down to consciously dredge for ideas. Nevertheless—and this is the important thing—these creative leaps aren't random or unpredictable; the fact that we can trace our steps back to that first spark shows that the steps are incremental, that there's a method and logic.

On the Subject

I was lying in bed one morning, worrying about what I was going to write next .... A poster of the Vermeer painting *Girl With a Pearl Earring* hung in my bedroom, as it had done since I was nineteen and first discovered the painting. I lay there idly contemplating the girl's face, and thought suddenly, I wonder what Vermeer did to her to make her look like that. Now there's a story worth writing. Within three days I had the whole story worked out. It was effortless; I could see all the drama and conflict in the look on her face. Vermeer had done my work for me.

—*Tracy Chevalier, on* Girl With a Pearl Earring

To illustrate, let's take a look at a fairly clear-cut exercise I sometimes bring in for my creative writing students to get them thinking about the way initial ideas suggest the larger story.

EXERCISE: BUILDING INITIAL IDEAS

Directions: Choose an attribute from Column A and pair it with a character type from Column B. What does a given combination automatically suggest to you about character and conflict? What about plot, voice, tone, approach, possible scenes, and images?

A	B
talentless	surgeon
suicidal	nun
kindhearted	circus clown
neurotic	suicide-hotline volunteer
unfulfilled	celebrity impersonator
scheming	department store Santa
racist	sports mascot
vain	supermodel
depressed	hitman
self-conscious	relationship counselor
jealous	serial killer

When I bring this exercise to a class, it usually takes on the feeling of a game, as it should. I ask students for combinations that stand out as interesting or compelling, and they call out whatever catches their attention so we can discuss it. "Racist suicide-hotline volunteer" once prompted forty-five minutes of discussion on its own, getting laughter at times and, at others, thoughtful silence. We'd come up with a pretty full picture of that twisted, pitiable character by the end of the discussion; maybe one day one of those students will write his story.

Occasionally a student will call out a combination that seems a likely fit and which, for that very reason, ends up being rather useless as grounds for fiction ... "kindhearted nun," for example, or "vain supermodel." When such an obvious pairing is made, other students usually chime in on why the pair won't work: We expect our nuns to be kindhearted, just as we expect our supermodels to be vain—we're speaking generally here—and thus there's nothing surprising or particularly interesting in the combination. We'd be writing caricature instead of character. There's little there to catch or keep our attention.

Sometimes a student will raise her hand and ask why Column A is such a bummer: racist, vain, suicidal, neurotic .... Would it kill me to make a column where happier things are going on? To which I respond: It wouldn't kill me, but it'd probably kill our story before it started. Fiction thrives on conflict, and a workable story idea is one in which the conflict is clear and present in the basic premise.

Again, "kindhearted nun" gives us nothing besides what we already know ... but what about *jealous* nun? Jealous of whom? Jealous over what, exactly, and what might this jealousy lead her to do? Maybe, and we're just thinking out loud, she's jealous of a younger nun in her convent and her closeness to God (and notice that as soon as we have a younger nun, our first nun becomes older). Back to the jealousy: Nuns are "married" to God, so it might be that the pretty young nun is in the role of the other woman, in some twisted sense. It's a crime of passion, dressed up like piety, and apparently there's a *crime* involved, or at least thought about, since we just used the word, though our tone was already pretty heavy from the beginning; this rivalry is getting out of hand. What's really irritating our older nun? Something about this young nun is touching a raw nerve with her ... wonder what exposed that nerve in the first place? (We'll have to think about this thorny older nun a little more, think about what's really going on in that habit of hers ...) What lengths might our jealous old nun go to in order to get rid of this woman she sees as a rival?

As we begin to ask and then answer these questions, the ideas, digressions, wrong turns, and occasional direct hits begin to form a story by addressing four basic problems:

1. What does the combination really suggest in terms of what might happen?
2. What would be motivating or driving our main character in such a situation?
3. What would be opposing the character in the situation? (This could, and probably should, prompt many different answers, some of them small and personal in scope, others large.)
4. What are the emotions evoked by or from the premise that we might consider universal? In other words, what could any reader identify with, regardless of whether or not she's ever been in this exact situation?

And there you have it: plot, character, conflict, and theme.

We also have a setting, which we'll want to do some research on (get thee to a nunnery!), and a tone, which is getting pretty dark. We also have a supporting cast to begin thinking about, most notably in the pretty young nun who knows she's being picked on by the older one but probably has no idea why or what kind of trouble she's inadvertently started. And we'll have many other nuns we can use to reflect and illustrate the main character's situation. What else comes to mind? What images? Stone archways? Meditation gardens? How creepy would a convent be at night, anyway? All those long, gothic, slinking shadows ...

Thus a full world begins to suggest itself to us, all from "jealous nun." True, this exercise is perhaps cheating a little bit. After all, no one is going to come up to you on the street and say, "Start writing about a jealous nun!" That's just a prompt you get in a writing book, right?

Except for that thing you saw at the convenience story today, those two women standing in line in front of you, if you were paying attention. Two nuns, a younger one with smooth skin and a bright smile who made a point of speaking to the cashier while they checked out, very friendly and bright, a musical voice that carried through the store. But there was something odd about the other one, the older nun, and the way she straightened her back whenever the young nun spoke, the funny way she had of clenching her jaw, almost as if she were embarrassed, or irritated, or ... could she have been angry? Or in some way jealous of the younger nun? And if so, What if ...?

KEEPING TRACK OF YOUR IDEAS

Once you start recognizing the story ideas that present themselves almost daily—and paying attention where they lead you—you'll want to keep track of them and recognize which ones might suggest workable stories. To that end, you'll want to engage in the following:

- **Keep a notebook.** Get in the habit of writing your ideas down in a journal so you'll remember them later. This should be something small and convenient enough to keep with you at all times; even a back-pocket-sized notebook will do. There will be times when an idea hits you when you can't write on a piece of paper, such as showering or driving to and from work. So please keep the idea in your head until you've stepped out of the shower or parked your car. (Along similar lines, story ideas especially like to show up right as you're drifting off to sleep. So keep a notebook, flashlight, and pen on your bedside, wake up, and jot them down. We're all guilty of thinking, *Oh, that's a great idea. I'm sure I'll remember that one in the morning.* Um, no. You probably won't. (For more practical tips for getting and working through story ideas, see Appendix A: Practical Tips for the Nighttime Novelist on page 228.)

- **Test your ideas.** When you come across a new story idea—or, if you already have an idea you're pondering—put it to the same kind of test as the example from the exercise that begins on page 8, seeing how the idea begins to bring up other elements of story (character, conflict, motivation, plot, setting, and so on). Does the initial idea or concept lead to these elements, building step by step? If not, can you figure out where the idea breaks down? Does the premise suggest a character? Does the character have a clear motivation? Does the motivation suggest a potential conflict in the story? And so on.

- **Exercise right.** For some practice on building a story from an initial idea, try doing the exercise on page 8 for yourself, addressing questions of character, motivation, plot, tone, and anything else that comes up. Don't censor or limit yourself at this point. Instead, write down anything that comes to mind about the potential story and see how long you can keep finding new ideas and directions in the premise.

WHERE TO LOOK FOR STORY IDEAS

It's true that story ideas will come to you if you learn to pay attention to what's going on around you and recognize those moments when your mind has begun to creatively wander. But there are also other ways, and places, you might look for inspiration when you need a boost.

First Lines. Sometimes a compelling story idea comes not from any conversation overheard, or anything you catch a glimpse of, but from a little voice that whispers a strange, interesting line in your ear … say, "I have always had an irrational fear of first kisses" or "Her husband had become hooked on daytime soaps" or "For as long as I'd known her, Jenny claimed that her dream was to become the ninth Mrs. Larry King." A good first line begins to suggest character, conflict, plot, tone, and theme the same way a compelling initial idea or image does. For example, what do you see present or suggested in the following first lines?

> In the town, there were two mutes and they were always together. (Carson McCullers, *The Heart Is a Lonely Hunter*)

> Mother died today. Or maybe yesterday, I can't be sure. (Albert Camus, *The Stranger*)

> Something is wrong in the house. (Kathryn Davis, *Hell*)

Headlines. A well-written headline contains enough possibility to get our imaginations working in the right direction (since the headline writer wants us to be intrigued enough to wonder about the story behind the headline and read it). For the fiction writer, we need not read the piece that goes along with a good headline—and in fact we probably shouldn't. Instead, the headline will make us want to know the story behind it and begin *writing* it. What really happened isn't as important to us as what might happen.

Here are a few real-world examples to consider, any one of which might suggest a sustainable story idea:

17 Burn At Same Time To Break Record

S.C. Cheerleader Hunts, Kills 10-Foot-Long Alligator

Game Show Looks to Convert Atheists

Jedi Thrown Out of Grocery Store

Already I can picture this poor middle-aged master Jedi, five days of stubble on his face, holding onto his box of Captain Crunch for life. "You don't want to throw me out," wiggling his fingers in the manager's face as he's pushed out the door. "You don't want to throw me out ..."

Titles. Sometimes inspiration for a book will begin before you've even hit the first chapter, with a title that starts you thinking. I suspect the reason for this is that good titles are often difficult to come up with, so when a good one comes along, it suggests possibilities immediately. Keep a page in your notebook just for title ideas. One of them might bring a story along with it.

Reading. At the risk of sounding obvious, good writers are first and foremost good readers. I realize that in our rushed lives—and this is especially true for the Nighttime Novelist, who has limited spare time and wants to use it well—it can sometimes be difficult to slow down, sit down, and enjoy a good book. But there can be nothing more instructive, nor more inspiring to your work, than reading a book from an author who does it right. (In fact, it often takes me longer to read a great book than a bad one, simply because every few pages I have to stop to jot down some idea inspired by the text.)

It's true that you might want to avoid other writers when you're in the midst of your own book, for fear of being influenced too much by what you're reading or losing the sound of your voice; that's a matter of personal preference. But reading consistently, and reading as a writer, can be a constant source of inspiration. Find writers you love, then find the writers they love. Reading is the best creative writing course you'll ever take.

Other Forms of Art. Finding beautiful art that speaks to you—no matter what kind—tweaks your artist's brain and opens you up for creative thinking. So, if you ever find yourself bereft of inspiration, go out and see a film that's been well reviewed, or rent a classic film you've never seen. Take a weekend trip to an art show or go browse the art books at the local bookseller. Put on that classic album you haven't heard in a while, turn down the lights, and really listen to it (rather than having it on as background noise while you run errands or try to get chores done). You'll likely find a few films, albums, or artists who particularly strike you, and to whom you'll go back many times in the course of your career for new inspiration. For me, the last ten minutes of Federico Fellini's 8½ does the trick. All those major and minor characters from the film joining hands and dancing around together like they're in the circus. Maybe it's the audacity of the ending I like best; seeing another artist unafraid of taking such a big risk encourages me to be brave in my own work.

WHY "WRITE WHAT YOU KNOW" IS POTENTIALLY BAD ADVICE

There are two pieces of writing advice that are so pervasive, so well known, that even non-writers have heard of them: "write what you know" and "show, don't tell." The problem is, both are to some degree misleading—and even potentially damaging to the creative process—if taken too literally. (We'll take on "show, don't tell" later, on page 151.)

In terms of your initial ideas and thinking about your story, "write what you know" can be tricky advice. The reason for this is in how most interpret the expression: "Write what I know? I'd better start thinking back to things that have happened to me in the past so I can write about them." Such a writer then begins reflecting on those personal moments that had an impact on him or her—purely personal and subjective moments that don't necessarily mean anything to anyone besides the person remembering.

All of us have had the frustrating experience of trying to explain something that aggravated us, or made us happy, or upset us, to someone who wasn't there, only to have our listener say "uh-huh" and glaze over. In such awkward moments, at least we have a surefire exit strategy: "Well, you just had to be there." But we don't have any such luxury

On the Subject

We write out what we don't know about what we know.
—*Grace Paley*

when we try to take our personal, subjective experiences and make use of them in the public form of the novel. The last line of your novel can't be, "Well, you just had to be there."

Mining our real life for fiction can be problematic: In life, things often happen for no apparent rhyme or reason, and, more than that, we often do things for no apparent reason, too. We act on impulse, behave in strange ways; we're contradictory, inconsistent, confusing, or confused. Thus, when we try to use our own, often-baffling personal experiences in fiction, the result can be confusing for a reader. (Why did the character behave like that? Why did that one character just smash a window with a bowling ball? I thought the character wanted [blank], but then she forgot all about it. And why did that one guy have a crowbar?) Fiction, unlike life, has to be logical, has to build in meaning for a reader, whereas life can be rather chaotic and disjointed.

But this isn't to say that we don't ever write what we know. In fact, every time we write we're bringing something of ourselves and our personal hopes, fears, and experiences to the text—in how we think about our characters and their experiences, how we think about the ways *we* would react or feel in a certain situation. This is how we connect with our characters and stories—by finding something familiar in their motivations and conflicts, something we've felt before that has a bearing on the work, then exploring that feeling in the context of your story—and this is how our readers begin to connect with our characters, too. Even if your story takes place on Mars, in the way-distant future, there'll be something about the characters' plight that is identifiably human. Finding that everyday human element, and using your own feelings and experiences to explore it further, is what takes a story from a series of things that happen to a complete and meaningful experience for both reader and writer. It's not a process of telling people what you already know but discovering what you know—and sometimes being surprised by what you find—through your characters. (This is a process we'll discuss more fully throughout this book.)

FINDING AN IDEA THAT'S "NEVER BEEN DONE BEFORE"

New novelists seem to have a particular hang-up about making sure their idea has "never been done before." If you have this worry, let me try and put your mind at ease: It's all been done before.

This might sound a bit depressing, at least initially, but once it sinks in you'll find it rather liberating. There is no completely new, 100-percent-unique plot idea. There is no undiscovered or unheard-of theme or motivation. As high-school English teachers used to say, and probably still do, all of literature might be boiled down to a half-dozen conflicts, and as far as motivations go, there are still just seven Deadly Sins (and maybe as many virtues). The point is that it's not the idea but the *approach* that makes a work original. The Western canon has no shortage of revenge stories, but there's still only one *Moby-Dick*. Bookstores are filled with coming-of-age novels—they could make a complete section of them, if they wanted—but Sue Monk Kidd's *The Secret Life of Bees* is not J.D. Salinger's *Catcher in the Rye* or Donna Tartt's *The Little Friend* or Stephen King's *Carrie*.

On the Subject

Whatever our theme in writing, it is old and tired. Whatever our place, it has been visited by the stranger, it will never be new again. It is only the vision that can be new; but that is enough.
—*Eudora Welty*

What makes your book different from every other book out there is that it's been written by you. It forms, and is formed by, a singular vision that's uniquely yours (even as a part of your vision has been informed by other people's visions, the books you've read, the literature that inspired you to write in the first place).

So don't get discouraged when you begin to think of books similar to yours, as you undoubtedly will, or when you discuss your story idea with someone who chimes in, without thinking, "Oh, it's like [blank]." Just nod your head and say, "Sorta." Because it probably is like a number of other books ... but it's also a particular product of your distinctive vision and voice, which is what makes the work important.

FROM INITIAL IDEA TO BOOK

A solid initial idea or inspiration suggests the whole scope of your book. That's not to say that your ideas about the book won't change as you write; they will and they should, evolving to solve problems and suggest new possibilities. Still, the initial idea should contain all of the basics to guide your work.

Going back to the story we saw emerging from our hypothetical example of "jealous nun," let's consider how to tease out the initial shape and scope of the book we might write from it.

Premise: An older, established nun fixates on a young nun who has joined her convent, projecting on the young woman her dissatisfaction with her own relationship to God that spirals out of control and becomes a mind game, with the old nun looking to discredit her rival … or worse.

Character (basic sketch): MOTHER AGNES: mid-fifties, severe, humorless, devout, authoritarian, slightly crazy; strict; loves God to the point of fanaticism; something in her past that explains her fanaticism? other incidents of her destroying young women's lives or careers? (careful to avoid cliché with her; do I like the name?!?) EXTERNAL CONFLICT: Running a convent, keeping it "pure," running "smooth." INTERNAL CONFLICT: Jealous of younger nun, directs her anger toward her, vows to dismiss her and maybe destroy her. Misdirected anger.

YOUNG NUN: named anything besides Mary; though maybe *Marianne?* Friendly, sincere, beautiful (her beauty an initial reason the Mother reacts to her?); devout, has a past she wants to atone for; will be manipulated by older nun; is she the main character? or the older nun? EXTERNAL

CONFLICT: Picked on by older nun, put through various "tests" really designed to get rid of her. Doesn't understand why she's been singled out but goes through with it, beating the old nun's attempts to dismiss her and forcing the old nun to more severe actions. INTERNAL CONFLICT: Wants to be devout, make up for whatever guilt she's carrying around (from where?) and so doesn't see she's being manipulated. Vulnerable.

OTHER CHARACTERS: Other nuns, of course; need to do research on hierarchy of convents; mention earlier women MA directed her anger toward?

Plot: Begin with Mother's severity, inability to speak to God, frustration; major plot points include introduction of young nun, increasing punishment and pressure from Mother Agnes, then convincing young nun she's a friend wanting to "help?" Have scene where Agnes asks young nun to reveal her sins? For blackmail? Mother Agnes schemes against young nun, fails to intimidate her, and then comes in close, tries to earn her confidence; we'll understand the danger; escalation of conflict; at some point the young nun will have to recognize the danger she's in and there'll be some sort of confrontation; is the big confrontation the end of the book? Or maybe Mother Agnes actually leads to the young nun's death?

Tone: Dark, certainly. Psychological suspense. Need to find ways to show this build-up in suspense in character, images, even setting.

Voice/POV: Somber voice to fit the tone. From Mother Agnes' POV? She's probably too close to be able to tell the story, same for young nun. 3rd person? Or 1st person, with another young nun watching what happens? Or remembering what happened?

Setting: Convent. Dark, gothic imagery. In the daytime a pleasant retreat, at night almost haunted, menacing, like eyes always watching you; statues and gardens; research living conditions and day-to-day.

Theme: Too soon to know. Something about what we're willing to do for "salvation"? To feel safe, forgiven? Even betraying our own character? Also maybe about power, the strong bullying the weak …

Title: Way too soon to know. How about *Mission?* As in the place where the action takes place, and it's the old nun's mission to destroy the young nun? The initiation period for a nun is called postulancy. Could that be a title? Or maybe *Postulant?*

Now, will these initial notes, this initial idea, be enough to sustain a novel? There's only way to know: Begin writing the novel. But at least you'd have a framework to go on based on the initial idea. (For help, you can find a worksheet just like the preceding outline on page 234 in the back of this book.)

By the way, if any of the terms above are throwing you off, or if you're not sure what they mean or how they fit together, don't worry: We'll be looking at each one in-depth in the sections to follow. Besides, right now isn't the time to begin fretting about, overthinking, or forcing the idea. What we're doing right now is playing, looking at possibilities.

try it out

BRAINSTORMING THE NOVEL

Try brainstorming your novel idea this way, making any notes that might be helpful on Worksheet 1 on page 234. Don't feel constrained by these notes; they're not written in stone and will likely change and evolve as you go. The point right now is simply to allow ideas to develop that might steer the work ahead. Record any thoughts/images/ideas that come from brainstorming your premise. If there's anything you're unsure about, or that's blocking you, consider what in the premise might be causing the problem. Or, read ahead to the discussions on the elements of craft and return to the worksheet with new ideas or perspectives as you need.

CHARACTER CONCEPTING

How readers connect with, and relate to, your characters is the true test of effective fiction.

It doesn't matter if your novel takes place in Victorian England or the Old South or Middle Earth or Mars; when we relate to a character, and see something of ourselves in the character's struggle, then we feel the danger right along with her, feel what's at stake in her quest, feel the same urgency. When the character fails in her quest, we feel the loss as if it were our own. And when the character prevails, we feel the lift in our own hearts. All good fiction, regardless of the genre, is ultimately character-based. And what makes a character real and relatable to us is *complexity*: The character has the potential for both good and ill, to do the right thing and the wrong thing, to succeed or fail, and it's the character's decision-making along the way that determines the outcome (and the reader's level of interest, hope, and involvement).

But here's the trick: Your characters' ability to develop as rounded, relatable, often-surprising human beings depends first on how you

On the Subject

The test of any good fiction is that you should care something for the characters; the good to succeed, the bad to fail.

—*Mark Twain*

set them up in terms of *motivation*. Complex characters aren't built on competing, conflicted motivations. Rather, complexity emerges when a character's clear-cut wants, goals, or desires come into conflict with, or are otherwise put at risk by, what happens in your story.

This is something beginning novelists, in particular, have a difficult time accepting. They'll believe that motivation should be a kind of psychological maze, the more branches and twists, the better. And rather than real complexity, what emerges is confusion, with a character never grounded enough to know what it is he wants (and as a result, the reader never knows, either).

The other big problem writers run into is the exact opposite: a character who seems to want nothing from the start, who is going through the events of the plot seemingly because there's nothing better to do. The reader gets the feeling the character would be just as happy walking out of the novel to find a bagel.

The events that unfold in your plot are *only* meaningful to the reader if they are, first and foremost, meaningful for your character, and for your plot to be meaningful to your character, the events must come into direct conflict with whatever it is he wants. But just because your character has a simple or clear-cut motivation, that doesn't mean that the *character* will be simple or clear-cut. Do you know what he is *really* willing do to achieve his goal? Do you know why the goal is important to him in personal—as well as public, professional, or practical—terms? What would the outcome be if he achieved his goal, or if the character *failed* to achieve it? These are questions you might not know the answer to until your character actually faces the conflict. And the decisions the character makes in such moments not only reveal his full humanity and complexity but begin to suggest, and to steer, the course of your novel.

CHARACTER: THE HEART OF THE NOVEL

In Cormac McCarthy's *The Road*, an unnamed father and son, survivors of some never-specified apocalyptic event, head south by foot in the hopes of finding some, *any*, more sustainable world than the wasteland around them. "Going south" is thus the stated, *external* goal of the two characters; it's what they hope to accomplish in the most basic sense. And the external conflicts they face along the way—from desperate individuals hoping to steal their few resources to roving gangs of marauders rumbling up the road in diesel trucks to the hostile, unforgiving terrain itself—all stand in the way of that goal.

Does stating and understanding the external goal and conflicts of the story reveal the gripping emotional experience of reading *The Road*? Absolutely not. The external goal and conflict are aspects of pure plot, the general "what happens." And the external motivation and conflict as stated here—characters wanting to get somewhere and being hindered—are familiar to us, forming the basic plotline of everything from *The Odyssey* to *The Wizard of Oz* to Charles Frasier's *Cold Mountain* to the Steve Martin movie

On the Subject

Find out what your hero wants. Then just follow him.
— *Ray Bradbury*

technique

25

Planes, Trains, and Automobiles. Reduced to these terms, the external motivation and conflicts of McCarthy's novel seem unremarkable. But *The Road* is a remarkable, even unforgettable, book, and what makes it so is the way the external motivation and conflict parallel, complicate, and deepen our understanding of the characters' *internal* motivation and conflicts.

We find hints of the internal motivation of the characters by looking more closely at the stated external goal: The father and son are heading south in the hopes of finding a more hospitable climate. But the bleak, unrelenting environment McCarthy sets up in the novel's opening pages—with its "ashen daylight" and "cauterized terrain"—makes it clear that there probably *isn't* any place untouched by the cataclysm; the burnt-out condition of the world seems all-encompassing. If this is the case, and their stated goal of finding a more inhabitable environment is *unattainable*, what's really keeping the characters (and story) moving forward, and why do we care?

If you've read the book, then you know the answer: The father is using the goal of heading south as a way of holding onto the slimmest idea of hope. And the reason he's doing this is simple: He's trying, against all conceivable odds, to keep his young son alive. This is the father's *internal motivation*, the reason the events in the book are meaningful to him and, as a result, meaningful to us.

What would you do to protect the life of the ones you love? Could you steal to keep them alive? Could you take a life? Could you keep one foot moving in front of the other when there is, in fact, nowhere safe on earth you can go? These are all questions of *internal conflict*, questions that, along with the internal motivation, make the *external* motivation and conflict matter. And these are also the questions we find ourselves asking as we read the novel; you need never have been in a post-apocalyptic wasteland to find something relatable, and heartbreaking, in the father and son's journey.

This connection to character and what's personally at risk was a crucial component of McCarthy's initial creative spark, as he revealed in an interview with Oprah Winfrey:

> My son John and I ... went to El Paso, and we checked into the old hotel there, and one night John was asleep, it was ... probably about two or three o'clock in the morning, and I went over and I just stood and looked out the window at this town. ... I could hear the trains going through and that very lonesome sound, and I just had this image of what this town might look like in fifty or a hundred years. I just had this image of these fires up on the hill and everything being laid waste, and I thought about my little boy.

What sparked the idea for *The Road* was nothing more than McCarthy's looking out his hotel window at the darkened city, and at that moment two things converged: First, he imagined the city burnt-out and decimated. Then he looked at his young son sleeping in bed and found himself wondering, if the world were in ruins, could he protect his son? From this seemingly simple wandering thought, *The Road* was born—an apocalyptic story and vision, but also from the very beginning the story of a father wondering if he were fully capable of protecting his child from the harsh world.

This is precisely the way our own novel ideas should start: not just with an external idea, conflict, and motivation, but with a resonant and relatable view of who the characters are, what it is they truly want, and what they would do to achieve it. Without considering your character in such terms, you run the risk of having a novel in which things happen but affect no one, and as a result the events will resonate with neither your reader nor you as the author. However, when an understanding of character informs and is at the heart of your work, you'll find that the world you've created is one that the reader finds engaging, terrifying, touching, but above all familiar.

THE CHARACTER ARC

Let's spend just a quick moment recapping the terms used in the previous section to make sure we understand them and how they work together to form the heart of a novel. There are two types of motivation and conflict: internal and external. External motivation is the character's stated goal, what it is he or she hopes to accomplish by the end of the story, and external conflicts are those events and circumstances that (sometimes literally) stand in the character's way. Both of these are aspects of plot and are easy-to-spot, necessary components of story. Internal motivation and conflict can be a little more difficult to see, as these are often more subtle. Internal motivation is what the character wants on a personal level, what matters to him or her—which the external motivation and conflict help reveal more clearly. Internal conflict consists of what doubts or fears stand in the way ... a realization of what's at stake for the character. These may sound a bit complex when stated this way, but when all of these work together in a story, they become difficult to separate from each other precisely because they all become aspects of the same thing.

By the way, please don't let any of this talk about motivation and conflict, internal and external, make you think we need psychology degrees to write fiction; what we're really talking about here is a *character arc*. In its simplest terms, character arc is about supplying a character with specific wants or goals and then putting obstacles in his or her way. And the degree to which the character is successful, or not, in achieving the goal tells us something about the character as a person and, ideally, tells us something about ourselves as readers.

Let's simplify this even more by showing the basic form of a character arc—wants, what stands in the way, and resolution—and looking at a few examples everyone should be familiar with even if you haven't read the books, as all of these stories have become part of the pop culture.

THE WIZARD OF OZ
Character arc: Dorothy Gale

WANT	WHAT STANDS IN THE WAY	RESOLUTION
External	External	External
To follow the Yellow Brick Road and find the Wizard of Oz, return home to Kansas.	The Wicked Witch, flying monkeys, a field of poppies, etc.	Finds Wizard, who can't help her. Learns from Glinda the Good Witch that she can return home by clicking her heels, could all along.
Internal (pre-twister)	Internal (pre-twister)	Internal
To find a place she feels at home and people she feels close to as family. (Wants to be somewhere else "Over the Rainbow" and gets her wish.)	Dorothy is an orphan living with her aunt and uncle on their farm … not sure if she fits in and is accepted.	Back in Kansas, realizes her aunt, uncle, and their farmhands are her real family. Realizes this is where she belongs. Realizes she's been "home" all along. That both "home" and "family" mean the people you love and who love you back.

THE SILENCE OF THE LAMBS
Character arc: Clarice Starling

WANT	WHAT STANDS IN THE WAY	RESOLUTION
External	External	External
To find and stop serial killer Buffalo Bill.	Bill's enigmatic clues and M.O.	Finds Buffalo Bill, has to face him alone, prevails.
To rescue Sen. Ruth Martin's daughter before she's killed. To convince Hannibal Lecter to reveal what he knows of Buffalo Bill and aid the investigation.	Racing against time. Lecter's mind-gaming "help."	Finds and saves Catherine Martin. Lecter's "mentorship" helps Starling solve case ... strange, equal relationship develops.
Internal	Internal	Internal
To prove herself worthy of being a full FBI agent.	Her self-doubt and inexperience.	Prevails, granted agent status, proves herself.
To escape the poverty of her past and upbringing and make something of herself. To save an innocent and stop the "horrible screaming of the lambs" from a traumatic childhood memory.	Being marginalized by the FBI and other law enforcement (especially for her gender and youth). Lecter's mind games revealing her fears and doubts.	Granted agency. Becomes full person. Puts her doubts and demons to rest. Until the sequel, anyway.

THE LORD OF THE RINGS (WHOLE TRILOGY)
Character arc: Frodo Baggins

WANT	WHAT STANDS IN THE WAY	RESOLUTION
External	External	External
To destroy the One Ring at Mount Doom.	Orcs. Ringwraiths. Giant spiders! Gollum. Etc.	Takes the Ring to Mount Doom and finally destroys it.
Internal	Internal	Internal
Not just to save the world, but to save *his* world, to preserve Hobbiton and the way of life he loves. His strength of character, which leads Gandalf to entrust the Ring to him.	Doubts about whether he, as a simple Hobbit, is up to the important task. The Ring's influencing Frodo's mind, tempting him, trying to manipulate him.	Faces severe temptation and prevails. Returns to innocence in a sense, but is nevertheless wiser as a Ringbearer.

You'll notice that in all of these character arcs—which closely parallel the novels' plot arcs, as we'll discuss more in Plot Planning on page 39—we really begin not with the external motivation but the internal: in Kansas with the lonely Dorothy, or at Langley with the student Clarice Starling trying to prove herself, or in the Shire with Frodo and the Hobbits, enjoying a way of life that's about to be put in peril. We begin with the internal motivation because it shows what's really at stake for the characters, which will be further revealed, and *tested*, by the external motivation and conflict when they appear.

DEVELOPING YOUR SUPPORTING CAST

Supporting characters better our understanding of the main character and the circumstances she finds herself in, whether long-term (I need to solve this homicide case) or the short-term (I need a ham sandwich). And if your supporting characters *aren't* working toward an understanding of the main character or situation in some way, you might ask yourself what they're really doing there, hogging time and space in your book. Your novel isn't an open house for complete strangers to walk through as they wish. Everything you spend time on must be for a reason, including those minor characters who *appear* to be simply passing through.

That said, your supporting cast can't seem like they're only hanging around to provide information or further the plot. Rather, your secondary characters, even the ones who appear in the book for only a couple of paragraphs and then are gone forever, must appear in those paragraphs as independent people with unique personalities, motivations, and desires of their own ... and you often have to accomplish this in just a few choice words or lines.

For example, let's start with a simple enough premise and conflict—a man and woman on an uncomfortable dinner date—and consider what that situation calls for in terms of supporting characters. They're at a restaurant and are unhappy with their relationship, for whatever reason, though the tension in the scene comes from their being unwilling or unable to express their unhappiness, from their silence and bottling it up. So a secondary character working with and against this problem might be a waitress who, unlike our two quietly suffering characters, comes over and tries to say everything. Who is simply trying to be cheery—and trying to make a sale—and whose fake outgoingness helps highlight our main characters' quiet desperation. The waitress might not pick up on the fact the two are having a fight of sorts and might start suggesting every dinner- or drink-for-two on the menu, clueless to the tension between them.

We'd find ways to deliver her character clearly from the way she speaks, acts, dresses—loud, overbearing, pieces of flair on her suspenders, lipstick on the tooth—and we'd see that she has a clear, simple motivation all her own: taking an order, and trying to push tonight's special. But her actions in following through with the motivation give us a way of seeing the *main* characters and their predicament in fuller, if depressing, terms. (Note, too, that we'd have even more minor characters in the scene—young couples in love, old couples in silence, an obnoxious kid's birthday party—and that all of them, even though rendered quickly, would be serving the same function of showing our suffering couple more clearly.)

This is the case for every minor character you make part of your cast, whether the character comes in once to fulfill a specific function and then leaves or becomes a *recurring* one, someone who plays an important role in building the story as part of a subplot (which we'll discuss further in Finding Your Subplots, beginning on page 49).

ROUNDING FLAT CHARACTERS

If you find yourself having trouble seeing your characters, whether major or minor, as full people in their own right, here are a few questions you might ask to help nudge them in the right direction.

What's the character's internal motivation; what does he or she really want? This might particularly be a question to ask of a flat protagonist, the result of a main character who seems motivated by nothing but plot-level or external circumstances. Remember that your hero is also a person like you or me … and consider what *we'd* feel in a similar situation. (And don't forget that even minor characters have motivations, and lives, of their own.)

How might you locate a character's internal motivation and conflict if these seem to be absent? If your character's motivation seems *purely* external, perhaps as part of his obligation or job—if you're writing a detective novel, and the character has simply taken on a new case—try to consider what it is about the character, personally, that informs his or her professional work, how it influences his ability to do the job, or speaks to the reason he entered this profession in the first place. Also consider how this particular job is different from yesterday's job, or tomorrow's, or last year's. Presumably part of what makes this job or case different is that it is *personally* different, there's something *personally* at stake. How might that be the case?

What peculiar traits—of appearance, personality, behavior, mannerisms, speech—might you highlight about the

character to make him seem fuller? I don't mean that giving a monocle and a handlebar moustache to a character automatically makes him full. Instead, consider what unusual or distinctive features might exist for your character naturally ... and might help us see him or her.

Are you playing both with and against type? No character is 100 percent good or evil, kindhearted or callous, capable or clueless, so consider not only how to set up our expectation of character but also how to subvert that expectation, how to complicate our view of a character. Hannibal Lecter would be a lot of fun to share a glass of wine with, discussing art and music and philosophy and the finer things. So long as he didn't kill and eat you.

How is the heart of the character, the motivation, evident in a work you admire? Consider this with any novel or work that means something to you, no matter the genre. Try looking back at the main character you find compelling and play armchair psychologist a bit, looking at how the external and internal motivation and conflict play with, or play off of, each other.

REVEALING CHARACTER

Writers reveal character—along with motivation and conflict—through a balance of showing and telling, by inspiring the reader to put himself into the story's situation, taking note of what he feels, imagines, sees, and hears.

If you know what's motivating your character in a particular scene and what's standing in the way in terms of conflict—every scene you write, by the way, contains its own arc of want, what's standing in the way, and resolution, even if the scale is small—how would you convey all of this simply through the way the character behaves? Through the way she speaks to other people? Through descriptions, language, pacing, even sentence length in the scene?

Think of the last time you were in a situation where you sat back and witnessed two people in some level of conflict. To stick with our earlier example, say out to dinner with a couple who was silently, sneakily fighting about something (hopefully you weren't one of the two, as this requires some objectivity). How could you tell they were bickering? What mannerisms did the couple take on that let you know that? What was it in their conversation, whether things said or left implied? Did the man keep sighing and checking his watch? Did his jimmying leg shake the table and make the ice clink in the water glasses? Did the woman make comments that seemed to be part of some conversation unrelated to ordering dinner? Did she add pet names to the end of everything, though the pet names sounded less than loving? As in, "You never know what you really want, do you, dear? You shouldn't order the steak, dear. You might choke and die. I'd hate for you to turn blue and choke and die, sweetie." (For a further lesson in this kind of text-and-subtext development of character, and for more vicious pet names, please see Raymond Carver's short story "What We Talk About When We Talk About Love." Then be thankful you've never gone to dinner with *those* couples.)

There are times when it's appropriate and necessary to reveal a character, motivation, and conflict directly, even stating these outright in a text (the infamous "telling"). But more often we reveal character in small, subtle ways that nudge the reader's view of the character and build meaning over time.

Let's try an exercise designed to get you thinking about the subtle ways we build character in a scene, beginning with an understanding of motivation and conflict and then considering how to convey these simply and effectively.

EXERCISE: **REVEALING CHARACTER**

From the lists below, choose a motivation for each of these two characters, a man and a woman, in a darkened theater waiting for a movie to start. Consider how the motivations you've chosen for them in some way put the two in a state of conflict, and think of how you'd convey these motivations and essential conflicts in subtle ways, without having the characters directly state what's bothering them. Think of anything that comes to mind: mannerisms, dialogue, the environment and its possibilities. Then, write a single page where you eavesdrop on and observe these two, allowing their unstated conflict to form the basis of a brief, complete scene.

	Man	Woman
	is having an affair	is embarrassed
	is thinking about something else	is thinking of leaving him
	is thinking of proposing	is still in love with him
	is oblivious	is in love with someone else
	is afraid he loves her more than she loves him	is anxious to go home
	is worried about money	is trying to reveal something important

MAKING A CHARACTER SKETCH

Thinking about the questions raised in the chapter, begin putting together your own main character sketch, using Worksheets 2 and 3 on pages 235 and 236. (If you get stuck, refer back to my examples—Dorothy, Agent Starling, and Frodo—beginning on page 29.) In addition to answering some of these baseline questions, you might also want to keep a list of keywords or images that jump out at you, even if these seem to be intuitive and don't yet make logical sense.

PLOT PLANNING

The basic structure of plot, like that of character, is considered an arc: Your protagonist has a clear goal or objective, faces direct conflict and challenges to that goal, and in the end either achieves the goal or is denied. Plot and character arcs run parallel to each other in the novel and help reveal one another, with the difference being that the character arc is about internal motivation, conflict, and resolution and the plot arc about *external* motivation, conflict, and resolution.

Chances are, the far ends of your plot arc are already clear to you; you know where the character's quest begins, and you know what the outcome will be. So the task becomes moving the character from the initial goal or motivation to the resolution in a way that's compelling and that seems, above all, unavoidable. You must build your story scene by scene, chapter by chapter, and continually raise the stakes so that the reader feels a sense of urgency along with the character.

It's sometimes said that there are really two kinds of novelists, the intuitive and the meticulous. The intuitive novelist has a sense of where

On the Subject

Writing a novel is like driving a car at night. You can see only as far as your headlights, but you can make the whole trip that way.

—*E.L. Doctorow*

the story is headed but leaves the particulars open to discovery—she knows where she'll end up but not necessarily how she'll get there—whereas the meticulous novelist keeps the journey mapped out and organized, using note cards of possible scenes and events, planning each new step, turning her writing space into something that looks like a crime lab littered in scrawled-out clues.

The truth of the matter is, most novelists are neither exclusively intuitive nor meticulous but somewhere in between. Out of the initial story idea springs overall character and plot arcs, as well as a few general key scenes, important turning points, or moments of conflict. But bridging these points, or specific markers, from beginning to middle to end is still something of a mystery, a process of discovery. We can see the next point we need to get to on the map, but we make the roads ourselves as we go, taking an occasional dead end or a long detour but hopefully staying on the most direct and interesting path.

FUNCTION OF PLOT:
THE OLD CAT & MOUSE

What drives fiction is conflict. But in terms of plot and structure, it might be more helpful to think of this as *suspense*.

An effective plot is a bit of a cat and mouse game in which the author builds suspense, rewards the reader by releasing it, and then re-raises it in new, unexpected, but nevertheless inevitable ways. Think of the plot of a mystery or detective novel as a good example. You begin a detective novel with a question (whodunit?) and usually one solid lead to go on that *might* provide the answer but only really provides *an* answer, momentarily releasing the tension or breaking the suspense by giving us a piece of the puzzle ... though the answer we get early on raises two more (related) questions. So we follow those leads, get what answer they have to offer and feel the tension momentarily release, then the suspense builds again as we follow the *next* set of questions. The mystery novelist will continue building, releasing, and rebuilding tension in this way until the middle-end of the book, when suddenly the answers we get stop raising new questions and go toward addressing earlier ones until we arrive, by the

On the Subject

Plot is the structure of revelation—that is to say, it is the method and timing with which you impart important details of the story so that the reader will know just enough to be engaged while still wanting to know more.

—*Walter Mosley*

end, at the answer we've been looking for all along, feeling that final release and the satisfaction that the case has been solved.

This is really what *all* novelists do in plot: We pose an overall question we'll need to answer in the book—will the protagonist achieve her goal?—leading to an overall answer. But along the way we use conflict to create miniature versions of the arc, posing minor challenges and smaller questions for the character to tackle, the resolution of each posing the next new challenge, goal, or question until we get to the end of the book and achieve our ultimate resolution.

SHAPING THE NOVEL: THREE-ACT STRUCTURE

One of the burdens of shaping a novel comes in balancing the macro and micro—giving full attention to the needs of the particular scene or moment at hand while also maintaining a momentum aimed at furthering the overall arc of the book. Of the two, the macro is often what gets neglected; the individual scenes or moments will be interesting on their own, but it's not always clear that these are advancing an overarching, unified plot. The result can feel episodic, like a collection of things that happen rather than parts of a whole building in logical, incremental, inevitable ways.

It's helpful, then, to have a clear conception of the macro—the novel structure as a whole—as a way of keeping your work focused and forward-moving and allowing yourself the *freedom* to focus on the small moments, knowing that these are working toward the larger goal rather than diverting from it. One of the best ways to think about overall structure comes to us from drama: the three-act structure.

In Act I, we have the Setup, introducing the character and his internal motivation, and we have an Inciting Incident, a moment of external conflict that reveals the extent of the internal conflict (what's really at stake for the character). Act I ends with a turning point called Plot Point 1, the external event (and motivation) that propels the character into the larger story.

In Act II we raise the stakes, as the character comes into more direct (and also indirect) conflict. The protagonist struggles to meet his external and internal goal and actually comes close to succeeding toward the middle-end

technique

of the act, at what's called the First Culmination, though he falls short. (We have a lot of story to go, after all.) When he gets close to his goal in the First Culmination and fails, this leads to the Darkest Moment, the point where it seems all is lost. But the character decides to make one last stand, to go all or nothing, a turning point called Plot Point 2, which ends the act.

In Act III, the protagonist faces the conflict head on, with everything he's hoped for and worked toward on the line, at the Climax (also called the Final Culmination) wherein the character either achieves his goal or not, no middle ground. What's left is the Dénouement, the winding down of story where the effect of what's been won or lost becomes clear to the character and reader.

Imagine the three-act novel structure looking something like this:

ACT I				ACT II			ACT III	
Setup	Inciting Incident	Plot Point 1		First Culmination	Darkest Moment	Plot Point 2	Climax	Dénouement
internal motivation revealed	external conflict that reveals stakes	turning point that reveals overall external motivation	escalating conflicts, building suspense	moment where protagonist is within reach of goal and fails	result of the failure of First Culmination, looks like all is lost	turning point when character decides to make last stand	moment where hero faces conflict directly, goes all in	winding down of action where effect of hero's win or loss becomes clear

Now, a word here: This information is offered as an aide, not as a set of inflexible rules. If you have a structure that fits the needs of your story and deviates from three-act form—and, of course, if your approach works—then by all means go for it. Nevertheless, when your initial idea started sparking key scenes and moments in your head, you were probably *already* thinking in terms of a three-act structure, whether you realized it or not.

STRUCTURING THE MICRO

Beginning with three-act structure—having these big-picture moments in mind and knowing what you're writing toward—allows you the flexibility to surprise yourself in how you get there, and the freedom to focus on and enjoy the smaller moments along the way. But there are also smaller, and no less important, organizing structures and strategies that will help you maintain unity and momentum in your work.

Chapters. Chapters are the most recognizable organizing structures of the novel, building the larger plot and character arcs while also containing completed arcs of their own. In fact, this is really the best way to describe what constitutes a single chapter: Chapters can be any size or length you need, so long as the chapter is a complete arc to itself, raising a particular problem at the beginning and answering it in some fulfilling way by the end. Keep in mind that a question you pose in a single chapter might be relatively small, same with the answer, though it'll raise a new question for the next chapter.

For example, the question posed by a single chapter might be, What does So-and-So know about thus-and-such?

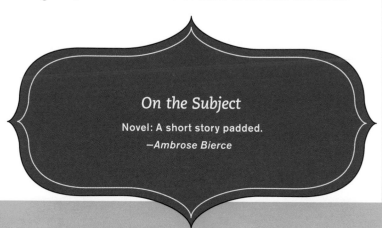

On the Subject

Novel: A short story padded.
—Ambrose Bierce

And the quest and conflict of the chapter might be to find So-and-So to ask him. A suitable resolution need not be finding the person and having him deliver a long, informative monologue; it might be going to the nursing home where you believe So-and-So lives, asking to see him, and having the attendant inform you, "So-and-So can't see you because he died in 1996, dummy." That certainly answers the question of the chapter, and thus the chapter is complete and fulfilled, even as the resolution raises *new* questions for the following chapters. Again, the old cat and mouse ...

Scenes. If chapters are the most recognizable organizing structure of a novel, scenes are the most basic and fundamental. A good scene—as you might guess I'd say—is itself a complete arc, raising a particular problem or goal and resolving it in a satisfactory way, though not every question or problem raised in a scene will be answered by the end of the scene; some will be left to answer in the next scene, or a later scene, or another part of the book altogether.

In the example from the previous point—going to see So-and-So—that chapter might contain the following scenes: first, an opening scene where we follow a lead about a missing girl that takes us to a bar, some place we're uncomfortable going in, to ask the bartender questions. Let's not say it's a biker bar, as that'd be too easy. Let's make it a senior citizens bar, rough crowd, and the conflict in that scene is that we're out of our element going into the place to begin with, as we're under eighty-five. As soon as we walk in, heads turn our direction, though maybe they're not looking at us because there's a TV over the door and *Matlock* is on.

And maybe we walk up to the bartender and do our best Sam Spade and ask him our question about the young girl who went missing and who wrote a check to this strange place a week before she disappeared, and in the FOR line all it said was "S&S." Did he know anything about that? And the hard-of-hearing bartender might ask, "Whaaa?" (This would go on for a while.)

But ultimately, after some doing, the bartender might reveal that S&S stands for "So-and-So," an old proprietor whose last-known address was Pleasant Oaks Retirement Center. So the conflict in this particular scene is getting this bit of information from a hard-of-hearing bartender who may or may not have a shotgun under the bar hooked up to The Clapper. How this scene plays out, and is fulfilled, leads us to the next scene (calling the family of the missing girl, maybe, to give them information, which will be a scene with its own conflict and arc) and the next scene (the phone conversation reminds the PI of an old memory, perhaps, and we go into flashback for a scene) before finally reaching the retirement community and the attendant who tells us the name we're pursuing belongs to a man who died during the Clinton administration—which gets its own scene with its own problems to face, of course—and that ends the chapter. (We'll discuss making effective scenes in more depth in Keeping Your Scenes Kinetic, beginning on page 171.)

Themes, motifs, and symbols. I'm speaking here not of big-picture theme, the overall "meaning" of your book—which we'll discuss in The Role of Theme on page 191—but of smaller recurring actions, events, or images that build important connections through their repetition. As writers we tend not to *choose* our smaller themes and motifs consciously—to say, for example, "Here's this bluebird again, and I tell you, it has meaning!" which generally a reader sees straight through—but instead we discover them as *we* see them repeating. At the moment when we discover such patterns and consider what they mean—when you realize, for example, that several chapters inadvertently use images of mirrors or reflections or shadows and these reveal your character's state of mind, as he's having trouble separating illusion from truth—you can begin to use these more consciously as a way of unifying the book. In this way, themes, motifs, and symbols are both a structural device, something that holds the novel together, and a substantive device, something that helps deepen the reader's understanding of story, character, and quest.

Subplots. We'll discuss these more in just a moment, but subplots are another way of structuring and unifying your novel. These occur in the novel the same way themes, motifs, and symbols do: intermittently and with a cumulative effect, building connections for the reader. Subplots are raised in some early part of the book, forgotten about as we turn our attention back to the main plot, and then reintroduced at intervals throughout, but each time the subplot comes back in, our understanding of it, and thus our understanding of the main plot and character, grows in some way. If the plot of a novel moves more or less in a straight line, then we might think of the movement of subplots, as well as themes, motifs, and symbols, as being circular, hitting at certain spots in the main plot and then disappearing from the linear plot, only to circle back around at some later time.

FINDING YOUR SUBPLOTS

This section is titled *finding*, rather than *making up some*, subplots because the best subplots typically arise out of your character's quest simply by having her face conflicts and come into contact with other characters. This is similar to how themes, motifs, and symbols emerge in a novel. When you try to intentionally insert a symbol into a story, it generally comes across as heavy-handed and forced. But, on the other hand, when you begin to notice that you've been using an awful lot of a particular image in different ways, then you've spotted something valuable; you might then figure out what it's doing in your book and begin using it consciously.

Same with subplot: When you try to force a subplot into a story where it doesn't belong—"I want the character's mother come in and boss her around; I think it'd be dramatic!"—the result is something that detracts and distracts. The reader can spot these kinds of subplots and generally tolerates them with a sigh: *Well, this'll be over soon and then we'll get back to that other part I liked.* But when subplot emerges as a natural part of the story you're telling, it becomes an indispensable and welcome part of the story rather than a diversion from it.

Subplot emerges when a particularly well-drawn secondary character (1) advances the primary plot and our understanding of it and (2) is enjoyable or rewarding in his or her own right, becoming so alive in that moment that you feel the need to revisit the character again and keep interacting. In other words, a subplot is a secondary relationship that helps us see the main character more clearly, one that continually comes into, recedes from, and reenters the novel in intervals. This is an important distinction to make: Not every secondary character is part of a true subplot, though every minor character in the book *should* allow us to see the main character and her quest in some new or better light.

Sometimes a secondary character will become *so* alive that he or she threatens to take over the story, and the subplot threatens to take over the plot. There are many worse problems to have than a character who pops into existence in this way, but keep in mind that all of your subplots exist to further the main plot and our understanding of the main character. And if the minor character is really insistent, tell her to be patient; maybe she'll get her own novel next.

Quick case in point: the Hannibal Lecter thread in *The Silence of the Lambs* is, if you can believe it, a subplot (and served the same function in Thomas Harris's earlier novel *Red Dragon*). The main plot of *The Silence of the Lambs* has to do with Clarice Starling facing her inner demons and doubts and, of course, hunting the serial killer Buffalo Bill, and the Lecter subplot furthers, and occasionally hinders, both of those. Nevertheless, we're pleased when the Lecter subplot comes into the book, not only because it's bettering our understanding of Starling and the Buffalo Bill story but because Lecter is such a fantastic presence ... and it's no surprise that Harris's next novel was called *Hannibal*, as the character had been auditioning for a starring role for two whole books.

Be on the lookout for those characters and relationships that suggest subplot, coming into the novel intermittently to sustain lesser but no less satisfying arcs of their own.

EXCISING POOR PLOT POINTS

Plot begins with a big-picture arc that includes (1) want, (2) what stands in the way, and (3) eventual resolution and then becomes more complex as we find new ways to explore and complicate that arc: paralleling internal and external arcs, putting major and minor conflicts in the protagonist's way, introducing secondary characters and subplots, and so on. And as we begin adding these new layers of complication—as our imaginations run more freely and our fingers fly across the keyboard—it can be easy for our novel, which started out tightly focused, to become cluttered, in a state of perpetual distraction.

If you feel your novel has begun to lose its forward momentum as a result of a plot that's got too much going on, you'll want to do what you can to get it back on course, beginning with looking at the following common plot problems and seeing which might be affecting your storytelling:

- *Mistaking inaction or digression for suspense.* The suspense required of an effective plot is about teasing the reader, true. But an effective tease isn't about intentional delay or digression, suggesting the character really needs to know something, or do something, and then having the character purposely not do or discover what's needed. Every scene in the novel must be active, even if the action is primarily emotional or mental, and each scene must seem like an attempt to solve the problem or question at hand. If you've set up that what the character needs to do is discover who rented the car that was found by the side of the road, and what the character does instead is go eat waffles, then the only suspense you've created is directed back to the author ... as in a reader wondering, "Why are we wasting time eating waffles?"

- *Mistaking character quirks for character deepening.* Back on page 35, we discussed how peculiarities of character—mannerisms, habits, behaviors—help deepen the reader's understanding and make our characters seem real and believable. But such quirks only feel real if they also feel relevant to the story in some way. It's great that your police sergeant enjoys classical music as well as NASCAR, is addicted to reality television, builds model airplanes, was a cheerleader in college, and operates HAM radio on the weekends, but perhaps be should be more concerned with that homicide ...

- *Mistaking minor characters and subplots for the main character and primary plot.* This is something we'll discuss in more depth in Overactive or Inactive Supporting Characters and Overactive or Inactive Subplots on pages 165 and 175, respectively. But the simple rule of thumb is that minor characters help us see the protagonist and subplots help us better understand the main plot. If some plot points don't lead back to these arcs, how might they? And if it seems they *can't*, maybe it's time to trim.

SKETCHING YOUR PLOT AND STRUCTURE

try it out

Look back at the information on plot and structure in this section and try to sketch out the basic, big picture arc and structure of your novel, thinking about which moments or scenes jump out as being key and how these suggest, or conform to, the traditional three-act structure (using Worksheet 5 on page 238). What you come up with here won't be set in stone quite yet, so don't fret too much. It's about finding a basic framework that'll allow you to visualize the overall shape, to think of key scenes, moments, and markers that define the story.

Make any kind of basic outline that suits you, any relevant notes or details that come to mind. Scribble on this arc, draw arrows, keep keywords in the margins corresponding to character or setting … do whatever is helpful and will keep you on track as you write.

NARRATION

I f you're thinking about narrative, you probably already have a basic idea of the character, motivation, and conflict of your novel, leading to the larger plot arc, some key scenes and turning points, and images or ideas that have affixed themselves to your imagination. You may also have begun to see overall theme and what it is you want to explore in the book, as well as discovered the tone and mood of the work. The question now becomes: How, exactly, do you begin turning these separate but related ideas into a novel? How do you start turning this blank sheet of paper in front of you into the complex world forming in your head?

The simplest answer is, one word at a time. Which is to say, you build your world, breathe life into your characters, create and release tension, and propel your reader through the events of your book all through narration.

Every fictional world you've ever been drawn into as a reader has been transmitted to you through a narrator telling you a story and, by his or her words, compelling you to believe it. Or maybe compulsion

On the Subject

When asked, "How do you write?" I invariably answer, "One word at a time," and the answer is invariably dismissed. But that is all it is.
—*Stephen King*

is too stern a word, sounds too much like an obligation, like jury duty; after all, a reader is someone who has volunteered to be part of this unwritten contract that says, basically, I want to believe this is true, so make me believe it. Perhaps a better way of saying it would be, A novelist uses narration, which is word-by-word storytelling, delivered through the visible or invisible presence of a narrator, to manipulate a reader into accepting that the people, events, and worlds described exist. But while in the real world it's generally frowned upon to manipulate people, as a novelist you don't need to worry; the only time your reader will be upset by your manipulating him will be when you do it poorly, or fail to do it at all.

On the other hand, when your narrative is focused, precise, and matches up with your intentions in the story, an interesting thing happens: Narration ceases to feel like something told to a reader and begins to feel like something experienced. This is accomplished, in part, by the use of specific detail and description that engage the reader's senses. But your success in creating and sustaining a believable fictional world begins with two fundamental and related considerations of narration: point of view, which is the narrator's relationship toward what's being narrated, and voice, which is the narrator's attitude toward what's narrated.

POV: KNOW YOUR OPTIONS

Point of view, or POV, has to do with the narrator's relationship to what's being said: Is the narrator a participant in the events being told, an observer of those events, or someone reconstructing the events from a distance? Does the narrator announce its presence openly or try to remain invisible? Is the narrator seemingly dispassionate and detached, or does the narrator have a clear opinion of, or stake in, the story? Is the narrator qualified to tell the story in terms of access to information and the ability to provide that information to us? And do we trust what's being said? All are questions you have to ask yourself of POV, as each kind opens up and allows certain freedoms in telling a story while limiting or denying others. The goal in selecting a point of view is not simply finding a way to convey information but being able to tell it the right way, making the world you create understandable and believable.

The following is a brief rundown of the basic forms of POV available to you and a description of how they work.

First-person singular. Characterized by the use of "I," this POV reveals an individual's experience directly through the

On the Subject

I had the first-person plural in mind from the beginning, but I switched back and forth and for a long while it was in the third person. Those were the novel's lowest days.
—*Joshua Ferris*

narration. This is the most common form of first person, with a single character telling a personal story and what it means or meant, how it feels or felt, to him or her. The information given is limited to the first-person narrator's direct experience (what she sees, hears, does, feels, says, etc.) and a certain degree of indirect experience (hearsay, conjecture, deduction, emotions, and anything else that has to do with interpreting or inventing information rather than witnessing it).

Pros: The first-person singular can make for an intimate and effective narrative voice—almost as if the narrator is speaking directly to the reader, sharing something private. This is a good choice for a novel that is primarily character-driven, where the character's personal state of mind and development are the main interests of the book.

Cons: Because the POV is limited to the narrator's own knowledge and experiences, any events that take place outside the narrator's observation have to come to her attention in order to be used in the story. A novel with a large cast of characters, or several crucial characters all doing and experiencing their own equally important things in different places, might be difficult to convey in a first-person novel, unless the narrator happens to be a voyeur, or a spy, or a psychic who can observe different people in different locations at once. (This is a joke. Please don't have a psychic first-person narrator who gets around this problem by saying, "I psychically intuited Bob was across town getting a haircut.")

Some examples of classic first-person novels include *Deliverance* by James Dickey, *The Bell Jar* by Sylvia Plath, *The Sun Also Rises* by Ernest Hemingway, and *The Catcher in the Rye* by J.D. Salinger (though this last might fall just as easily into the unreliable narrator category, as we'll discuss momentarily).

Here's a sample opening line, from *The Bell Jar:* "It was a queer, sultry summer, the summer they electrocuted the Rosenbergs, and I didn't know what I was doing in New York."

First-person plural. Characterized by the use of "we," this POV uses a collective of individuals narrating as one. This is far less common than the first-person singular, but it can be powerful in that it combines the personality and intimacy of first person with some of the abilities of omniscient third person. This is a POV you might use when a community endures some common experience and begins relating it, trying to understand it as a group. The ready example is William Faulkner's short story "A Rose for Emily" in which the fictional town of Jefferson, Mississippi, comes to terms with the eccentric life, death, and secrets of its most unusual citizen, Miss Emily Grierson, a holdover from an Old South that no longer exists. Note the communal, even gossipy, feel of the opening line of the story, fueled by the town's morbid curiosity about the reclusive old woman:

> When Miss Emily Grierson died, our whole town went to her funeral: the men through a sort of respectful affection for a fallen monument, the women mostly out of curiosity to see the inside of her house, which no one save an old man-servant—a combined gardener and cook—had seen in at least ten years.

Pros: Behaves like first-person singular in its personality and subjectivity but also like third-person omniscient in that it's made up of not one person but many, able to witness more than a single person could. Individuals pop out of the "we" to provide needed information and then recede back into the collective.

Cons: Still a first-person voice and thus limited to the direct experiences of the members of the collective. It can also become tedious with the constant collective presence, so the author should take care to utilize both the intimate and public aspects, even letting the reader occasionally forget that the story is first person and not the more expansive third.

Some contemporary examples include *The Virgin Suicides* by Jeffrey Eugenides and *Then We Came to the End* by Joshua Ferris. The latter novel begins with this line: "We were fractious and overpaid. Our mornings lacked promise. At least those of us who smoked had something to look forward to at ten-fifteen."

First-person observer (aka first-person minor). This is a first-person narrator telling the story of someone who is incapable, for whatever reason, of telling his or her own story. Most often the incapacity is a matter of bias, mental or emotional duress or disability, or the main character's death, so the first-person observer tells the protagonist's story as he or she understood and witnessed it.

Though this, too, is a rather infrequent POV, there are nevertheless several classic examples in literature: *Moby-Dick* is told not by Ahab but by Ishmael; *The Great Gatsby* is told not by Gatsby but Nick Carraway. Not only are Ahab and Gatsby too deluded to tell their own stories—Ahab by his need for vengeance, Gatsby by his pretending to be someone he's not—but they both end up dead in the course of their novels, which naturally means they cannot narrate their own stories, since the last line of their books would be "Agh! I'm about to di—!" Lucky for them, the first-person observer has the distance and perspective to tell the protagonist's story, and also to comment upon the protagonist's story as needed.

Pros: It has the closeness and intimacy of first person but also the required distance to tell the story of a character not capable, for whatever reason, of telling his own story.

Cons: It allows interiority only for the narrator, not the protagonist proper, which calls for occasional conjecture as to what's happening in the protagonist's head. It also requires the narrator to be a character in the story but not to step up as the main character; he must be active enough to be present but passive enough not to get in the way of the main character and plot.

Besides *Gatsby* and *Moby-Dick*, the novella *Rita Hayworth and Shawshank Redemption* by Stephen King and the novel *A Prayer for Owen Meany* by John Irving are good examples.

Irving's novel begins:

> I am doomed to remember a boy with a wrecked voice. Not because of his voice, or because he was the smallest person I ever knew, or even because he was the instrument of my mother's death, but because he is the reason I believe in God. I am a Christian because of Owen Meany.

First-person unreliable (aka the unreliable narrator). If first-person observer is the POV to adopt when you want to work around a protagonist incapable of telling his own story, the unreliable narrator is the POV you choose when you want that character to tell his own story anyway, when the narrator's inability to accurately or "objectively" tell his story is part of what you want to explore.

It's not that the unreliable narrator knows he's being unreliable or is trying to deceive the reader; rather, the unreliable narrator believes he's telling the story straight, and it's the reader who realizes this isn't the case by picking up subtle, and sometimes not-so-subtle, cues. In this sense, the reader has a better understanding of the unreliable narrator—and more perspective to judge the story being told—than the narrator himself does. The classic example comes from Edgar Allan Poe's short story "The Tell-Tale Heart" in which the unnamed narrator explains and defends (defensiveness is one of the red flags of unreliability) his murdering of an old man whose sole offense seems to have been having a creepy, milky, "vulture-like" eye. By the second or third time the narrator claims to be completely sane—"Madmen know nothing. But you should have seen me!"—the reader understands that the narrator is batty ... the exact opposite of what's being told to us.

It should be said, though, that it's pretty rare to have an unreliable narrator as far gone as Poe's. More often the unreliability comes in degrees, and sometimes with the narrator admitting unreliability, which has the strange effect of somehow making the reader trust the narrator again.

Pros: This sophisticated POV has a kind of double reward for the reader: the level of story being told, and the level of story that the reader recognizes as being truer. This allows an author to explore dualities and levels of meaning not just in looking at truth vs. deception but, say, love vs. obsession (Vladimir Nabokov's *Lolita*) or "civilization" vs. real humanity (Mark Twain's *Huck Finn*) or whatever the subject.

Cons: When there's no compelling payoff for a reader in terms of revealing larger themes or ideas—or when unreliability stems from lying, withholding information, or toying with or taunting a reader—the unreliable narrator can actually work against your aims in a novel. Remember that an unreliable narrator works because it illuminates and broadens a reader's understanding of character and subject, not obscures it. So use this POV with caution and care, and begin by looking at novels in which the unreliable narration is revelatory.

Some classic examples include the aforementioned *The Adventures of Huckleberry Finn* by Twain and *Lolita* by Nabokov; contemporary novels that use an unreliable narrator include *The Virgin Suicides* by Jeffrey Eugenides and *The Curious Incident of the Dog in the Night-time* by Mark Haddon. Many of you may remember this colorful and compelling opening, delivered by Huck Finn:

> You don't know about me, without you have read a book by the name of **The Adventures of Tom Sawyer**, but that ain't no matter. That book was made by Mr. Mark Twain, and he told the truth, mainly. There was things that he stretched, but mainly he told the truth.

Second person. The second person takes as its main character "you," telling us what you do or who you are ("You walk to the sink and brush your teeth.") or sometimes coming in the form of commands or instructions ("Walk to the sink. Brush your teeth."). You'll more frequently see this POV used in short stories, where there's less room for error and redundancy; it can be especially difficult to sustain in a longer work for two (related) reasons: the novelty might be distracting for a reader in the long run, and the reader might rebel against being part of the narrative in the way the POV suggests, thinking to himself as the narrative orders him around *No I don't. No I don't. No I'm not … .*

Nevertheless, the second-person can create an unusual relationship between reader and text: On the one hand, the "you" character is always a distinct personality unto itself, with traits, motivations, and an identity all its own, but on the other hand, the reader slowly begins identifying with, and feeling close or even equal to, that persona. The character is separate from us but also the same. This can be particularly effective when we're faced with a character who is in some way flawed and who we might be inclined to dismiss in the first person or the third. It's more difficult to dismiss such a character in the second person because the character is, to some degree, you.

Pros: This POV creates a close bond between reader and character, with the second-person character both its own autonomous entity, separate from us, and at the same time an entity we identify with and feel equal to. This unusual relationship between reader and character—and the novelty of the voice and how it functions—can be interesting and engaging when it works.

Cons: The novelty of the voice alone isn't enough to sustain a full novel. The second person must also be purposeful, bringing us in close to a character or situation that we might not automatically feel close to or identify with in other POVs; we believe it in the second person because it happens to us.

Examples include the novels *Bright Lights, Big City* by Jay McInerny, *If on a winter's night a traveler* by Italo Calvino, and *Half Asleep in Frog Pajamas* by Tom Robbins, as well as the short story collection *Self-Help* by Lorrie Moore.

Calvino's novel begins:

> You are about to begin reading Italo Calvino's new novel **If on a winter's night a traveler**. Relax. Concentrate. Dispel every other thought. Let the world around you fade. Best to close the door; the TV is always on in the next room.

Third-person limited. This POV is characterized by the use of "he" or "she" and the character's name, as in, "John hated math. He hated it immensely." Unlike third-person omniscient, the third limited spends the entirety of the story in only one character's perspective, sometimes as if looking over that character's shoulder and sometimes going inside the character's mind, and the events are filtered through that character's perception (though less directly than first-person singular). Thus, the third limited has some of the closeness of first singular, letting us know a particular character's thoughts, feelings, and attitudes on the events being narrated, while also having the ability to pull back from the character to offer a wider perspective or view not bound by the protagonist's opinions or biases, thus being capable of calling out and revealing those biases (in often subtle ways) and showing the reader a clearer way of reading the character than the character himself would allow.

Pros: It offers the closeness of first person while maintaining the distance and authority of third and allows the author to explore a character's perceptions while providing perspective on the character or events that the character himself doesn't have. It also allows the author to tell an individual's story closely without being bound to that person's voice and its limitations.

Cons: Since all of the events narrated are filtered through a single character's perceptions, only what that character experiences directly or indirectly can be used in the story (as is the case with first-person singular).

Some famous examples include: *Herzog* by Saul Bellow, *Fahrenheit 451* by Ray Bradbury, *The Old Man and the Sea* by Ernest Hemingway, and the Harry Potter series by J.K. Rowling. Bellow's novel begins: "If I am out of my mind, it's all right with me, thought Moses Herzog."

Third-person omniscient. Characterized by the use of "he" or "she," and further characterized by having the powers of God, this POV is able to go into any character's perspective or consciousness and reveal his or her thoughts; able to go to any time, place, or setting; privy to information the characters themselves don't have; and able to comment on events that have happened, are happening, or will happen. The third-person omniscient voice is really a narrating personality unto itself, a kind of disembodied character in its own right—though the degree to which the narrator wants to be seen as a distinct personality, or wants to seem objective or impartial (and thus somewhat invisible as a separate personality), is up to your particular needs and style.

The third-person omniscient is a popular choice for novelists who have big casts and complex plots, as it allows the author to move about in time, space, and character as needed, though this is also a potential drawback of the voice: Too much freedom can lead to a lack of focus, spending too many brief moments in too many characters' heads so that we never feel grounded in any one particular experience, perspective, or arc.

Here's a good guiding principle: As a general rule, each chapter—and perhaps even each individual scene—should primarily focus on one particular character and perspective. Imagine how exhausting it would be to read a scene with five characters sitting around a table, each with something to hide, and the narrative moving line by line into each character's shifty mind: "I wonder if Johnny knows about Bob?" "Kay is looking at me funny. I wonder if she knows what Johnny knows." "If only Johnny knew that I know about Bob and Kay." "I'm Kay and I'm not sure why everyone is looking at me and Bob." Yikes. So you want to use the powers of the POV selectively and for a reason, without abusing those powers. In other words, don't use the freedom of omniscience as a substitute for, or as a shortcut to, real tension, drama, and revelation.

Pros: You have the storytelling powers of God, able to go any-where and dip into anyone's mind-set or consciousness. This is par-ticularly useful for novels with large casts and where the events or characters are spread out over, and separated by, time or space. A narrative personality emerges from third-person omniscience with the narration becoming a kind of character in its own right, able to offer information and perspective not available to the main charac-ters of the book.

Cons: Jumping from consciousness to consciousness—especially as a shortcut to dramatic tension and revelation—can lead to a story that is forever shifting in focus and perspective, like a mind reader on the fritz. To avoid this, consider each scene as having a particular character and question as its focal point and consider how the per-sonality that comes through the third-person omniscient's narrative voice helps unify the disparate action.

Some examples include: *The Lord of the Rings* by J.R.R. Tolkien, *One Hundred Years of Solitude* by Gabriel Garcia Marquez, *White Teeth* by Zadie Smith, and *Jonathan Strange & Mr. Norrell* by Susanna Clarke.

Clarke's novel begins:

SOME YEARS AGO there was in the city of York a society of magicians. They met upon the third Wednesday of every month and read each other long, dull papers upon the history of English magic.

MAKING THE RIGHT CHOICE FOR YOUR STORY & GENRE

To a certain degree we don't really choose a POV for our project; our project chooses POV for us. If we were writing a sprawling epic, for example, we wouldn't choose a first-person singular POV, with our main character constantly wondering what everyone back on Darvon-5 is doing. If we were writing a whodunit, we wouldn't choose an omniscient narrator who jumps into the butler's head in chapter one and has him think, *I dunnit*. Our story tells us how it should be told, and once we find the right POV and approach, we realize our story couldn't have been told any other way.

Hopefully the previous section gives you a good idea of how to match up POV with the aims you have for your story and the particular needs of your chosen genre. If you're still not sure, then you might want to take a look at the following chart to see if the questions and answers begin revealing the point of view needs of your novel.

On the Subject

Language forces us to perceive the world as man presents it to us.
—*Julia Penelope*

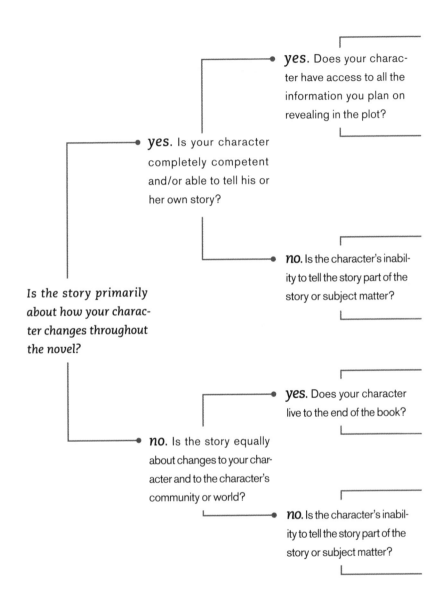

yes. Does your character have access to all the
information you plan on
revealing in the plot?

yes. Is your character
completely competent
and/or able to tell his or
her own story?

no. Is the character's inability to tell the story part of the
story or subject matter?

Is the story primarily
about how your charac-
ter changes throughout
the novel?

yes. Does your character
live to the end of the book?

no. Is the story equally
about changes to your character and to the character's
community or world?

no. Is the character's inability to tell the story part of the
story or subject matter?

●— *yes.* Try first-person singular

┌────────────────●— *yes.* Try third omniscient
●— *no.* Are other characters
and their experiences
needed to reveal the full
scope of the story?
└────────────────●— *no.* Try third limited

●— *yes.* Try first-person unreliable

●— *no.* Try first-person observer

●— *yes.* Try first-person singular or third limited

●— *no.* Try third limited

●— *yes.* Try third omniscient

┌────────────────●— *yes.* Try first-person sin-
●— *no.* Are the changes to the   gular or third limited
external world felt primarily
by your protagonist?
└────────────────●— *no.* Try third omniscient

It should be said that the preceding chart is unscientific, or maybe trying to be *too* scientific to contain something as fluid and mysterious as narrative, as not every problem can be anticipated and answered here. But at a baseline this illustrates the thought process and questioning that goes into choosing your POV.

FROM POV TO VOICE

If point of view is about the narrator's relationship to what's being said, voice is about the narrator's *attitude* toward the narrated, revealed not just in what is said but how it's said. If you go back and look at the sample first sentences in the POV: Know Your Options section, you'll see that each contains two levels of meaning, what's commonly referred to as story and discourse. Story is the basic plot-level information given to us in a line; discourse, the particular attitude conveyed toward what's given, which comes through *how* the information is given. In other words, story provides information, and discourse provides a way of reading and understanding the information.

Voice is about discourse, the *how* it's said that makes meaning for the reader and which is achieved through the following:

- *Perspective:* The sum feelings or thoughts of the narrator, protagonist, or both toward the subject being narrated

- *Tone:* The attitude toward that subject as revealed in word choices of the narrator/protagonist

- *Language:* The word-by-word choices—having to do with syntax, diction, line length, rhythm, etc.—that reveal the tone and perspective of the narrator, protagonist, or both

As you can see, these are closely related and dependent upon each other, though they're not the same things.

going deeper

Let's say a particular narrator's perspective toward the events he describes might be one of dislike or disdain … but what does that mean for the tone of the piece? Our first and most obvious reaction would be to say that the tone will be "disdainful," though this isn't very helpful and doesn't make a lot of sense. Do we mean that the tone will be angry, bitter, agitated? Or that it'll be sad, mournful, full of resignation? Wouldn't each one of these lead the voice in a slightly different direction? Besides, our initial impulse of a serious or sad voice might be off the mark altogether; the tone might be funny or satirical, showing displeasure with the subject by poking holes in it. So attitude toward the subject, plus a particular tone, begins forming voice—and these particulars are revealed through the language of the narrator (or protagonist, or both) and its nuances, goals, or limitations.

A quick word about this narrator/protagonist/both business: This depends upon the POV you've chosen and the narrator's relationship to the text. If you've chosen a first-person singular voice, then the attitude coming through in the voice clearly belongs to the protagonist (who is also the narrator). If you've chosen a third-person limited voice, then the attitude belongs to both the narrative presence and the protagonist (as revealed through the voice's occasionally entering the protagonist's head and then backing out). If you've chosen a third-person omniscient POV, then the attitude might still belong to both narrator and protagonist, though the narrator will be much more up front, as your cast of characters is likely large and spread out (thus your narrator's perspective is what unifies the action).

Let's take a look at a few examples to see how the POV changes our thoughts on whose perspective we're getting and to identify the perspective, tone, and language choices that make up voice.

To begin, let's look at the first-person singular narrator of Raymond Carver's short story "Cathedral":

This blind man, an old friend of my wife's, he was on his way to spend the night. His wife had died. So he was visiting the dead wife's relatives in Connecticut. He called my wife from his in-laws'. Arrangements were made. He would come by train, a five-hour trip, and my wife would meet him at the station. She hadn't seen him since she worked for him one summer in Seattle ten years ago. But she and the blind man had kept in touch. They made tapes and mailed them back and forth. I wasn't enthusiastic about his visit. He was no one I knew. And his being blind bothered me. My idea of blindness came from the movies. In the movies, the blind moved slowly and never laughed. Sometimes they were led by seeing-eye dogs. A blind man in my house was not something I looked forward to.

The attitude here is the protagonist's, the main character telling the story, and it's also a rather poor one. We know that the narrator/protagonist isn't happy about the blind man coming to his house because he tells us so, of course, but where is the first time this is evident to us, where we first understand the narrator's perspective on the events he's describing? The very first word: not *a* blind man but *this* blind man, which automatically reveals the narrator's defensiveness and discomfort (his perspective as well as his tone).

There's a good amount of story in the paragraph—filling in some information—but what we take away from the paragraph is primarily discourse, the narrator's attitude about this visit, which informs the reader's attitude about *him*. Furthermore, we know that not only is he on the defensive, but he's also not the brightest bulb, which we get through the short, straightforward, rather uncomplicated sentences (not to mention his simplistic and apparently unashamed dislike of "this blind man"). Were we to keep going in the story, we'd see more support for our early conclusions about this narrator, but we neverthe-less get a good sense even from the first paragraph. We're grounded in a clear voice, and already we have thoughts about the person at-tached to it.

For an example of voice from the third-person limited POV, take a look at these opening passages from Flannery O'Connor's story "A Late Encounter with the Enemy" (I've omitted a couple of bridging sentences and paragraphs for brevity):

> General Sash was a hundred and four years old. He lived with his granddaughter, Sally Poker Sash, who was sixty-two years old and who prayed every night on her knees that he would live until her graduation from college. The General didn't give two slaps for her graduation but he never doubted he would live for it. … A graduation exercise was not exactly his idea of a good time, even if, as she said, he would be expected to sit on the stage in his uniform. She said there would be a long procession of teachers and students in their robes but that there wouldn't be anything to equal him in his uniform. He knew this well enough without her telling him, and as for the damn procession, it could march to hell and back and not cause him a quiver …
>
> … For his part, the General would not have consented even to attend her graduation if she had not promised to see to it that he sat on the stage. He liked to sit on any stage. He considered that he was still a very handsome man. When he had been able to stand up, he had measured five feet four inches of pure game cock ….

The third-person limited means that we're getting some combination of the narrator's perspective on things and the protagonist's, as his thoughts occasionally come through in the text. And it's clear that the narrator in O'Connor's story has a different take and perspective on the events than the superannuated General Sash. The general's attitude is obviously one of pride, though the reader understands that the General's pride is closer to vanity, and undeserved. Occasionally we'll get the protagonist's thoughts and attitudes coming through the voice: that he didn't give two slaps for the whole thing, that the damn procession could march to hell, and that he only consented to being there because he likes being "on any stage." But the sly commentary coming through in the voice—in the narrator's attitude about the subject—shows that Sash is a rather ridiculous, self-absorbed old man, made most clear in the wonderful discrepancy in the last line quoted, that when he stood up (when he still could) he measured a mere five feet four inches of "pure game cock." We understand the protagonist's perspective and crotchety nature, but it's the juxtaposition of these with the *narrator's* perspective on Sash, the darkly comic and even satirical tone, that really makes meaning and establishes the voice of the piece.

Looking back at the example of Susanna Clarke's *Jonathan Strange & Mr. Norrell* and its use of third-person omniscient POV, again we see a clear voice and attitude, though the attitude belongs to the storytelling narrator:

> SOME YEARS AGO there was in the city of York a society of magicians. They met upon the third Wednesday of every month and read each other long, dull papers upon the history of English magic.
>
> They were gentleman-magicians, which is to say they had never harmed anyone by magic—nor ever done anyone the slightest good. In fact, to own the truth, not one of these magicians had ever cast the smallest spell, nor by magic caused one leaf to tremble upon a tree, made one mote of

dust to alter its course or changed a single hair upon anyone's head. But, with this one minor reservation, they enjoyed a reputation as some of the wisest and most magical gentlemen in Yorkshire.

The straight-up story in these opening paragraphs is fairly uncomplicated: We have a group of magicians who come together once a week to discuss magic. That's the basic information. But we know a lot more about them through the way the information is given: that they're academic rather than practical and are, in fact, rather feckless, men who would rather think about something (here, magic) than do it.

But do we presume that the magicians believe themselves to be ineffectual? Do we think that the magicians believe their papers to be "dull"? That they're aware of the fact they've never done "the slightest good" or never so much as "changed a hair upon anyone's head"? No. This is not the characters' attitudes about themselves but the narrator's attitude ... but it quickly becomes the reader's attitude, too. Because of the discourse—how it's said and the attitude toward the subjects—we begin to extrapolate, picturing these magicians in their musty occult libraries and their clawfoot chairs dressed in ridiculous old robes, smoking pipes, snifting brandy, seeming more like a Kiwanis meeting than a concert of alchemists. In other words, we already know quite a lot about them, and how to feel about them, just from how this is told.

What else would we say about the voice? For one, it's behaving like an old-fashioned storytelling presence, right down to the capitalization of SOME YEARS AGO, putting us in mind of storytelling presences we might find in fairy tales. But the mock formality of the tone and the word-by-word choices in language come across as humorous here, almost subversive: The narrator finds the men pompous and puffed up, and the voice subtly reveals that. Thus we have a clear voice with a personality and slant of its own luring us into the story but also telling us how to read it. How it's said is every bit as important as what is said.

EXERCISE: THE IMPORTANCE OF VOICE

Directions: Choose one of the passages from the section above—Carver, O'Connor, or Clarke—and rewrite the passage using the voice from one of the other examples. (For instance, retell the opening passage of *Jonathan Strange & Mr. Norrell* with Carver's narrator doing the narrating.) Read the voice you'll be appropriating several times out loud to yourself, to get a sense of its perspective, tone, cadence, language, and so on. In fact you might want to find a copy of the story and read larger portions of it out loud, to make sure you have a full sense of how the voice fits in your mouth. Then rewrite the scene you've chosen using the mismatched narrator, trying to tell it as that narrator would. The purpose of the exercise is to illustrate that, even with the same basic information being conveyed, differences in how it's told lead to a different story and experience altogether.

FINDING YOUR VOICE

We've already seen the importance of finding and establishing a narrative voice that fits your needs for the novel, matching up with and building off the POV and conveying a certain attitude toward the characters and events that the reader needs in order to fully understand your story. But what happens if the voice required by your story isn't necessarily one you feel comfortable with? What happens when you find yourself wrestling with voice, even after you've discovered the right one?

This goes directly to one of those persistent, pervasive pieces of advice you'll hear given to beginning novelists, the dreaded "find your voice." But does that mean something different than finding the voice that your novel requires? Is there a distinction to be made between the novel's voice and *your* voice? Or are they the same thing?

This is a difficult question to answer, not because there isn't a clear answer but because the answer is not always one beginning novelists want to hear: You have natural narrative tendencies, the beginnings of voice, already within you, made up of certain proclivities in storytelling, ways of seeing and saying that make sense to you and come to you more easily than others ... and these aren't always the ways of seeing and saying you wish they were.

Occasionally a writer will set out to work on the kind of novel he admires, only to realize later in the project that the kind of novel he admires isn't necessarily one he can write. You might have a good understanding of how the type of story works, and you may've read a million novels that do something similar, but understanding the approach doesn't always mean that it's one that will work for you. This is especially the case with those writers we idolize most; part of the reason a writer becomes a hero to us is that it seems like nobody does it like that person, that the author can't be emulated. And then, like Don Quixotes chasing down windmills, we set out to do just that, to emulate the writer who can't be emulated, sometimes spending years pursuing someone else's vision rather than considering our own.

This is something I struggled with early in my writing career, trying to emulate writers I loved whom I had no business trying to emulate; my natural tendencies weren't consistent with theirs. I assumed this was my own problem, that no other writers would be silly enough to fall into the same trap, but I quickly learned that this is common to the apprentice stage of writing. Everyone starts out trying to write like someone else, and eventually, through trial and error, we begin to realize what aspects of others' writing make sense to us and why, which parts make no sense to us and why. The better our understanding of what we aren't inclined to do as novelists, the better our understanding of what we *can* do, what works for us and makes sense. And through this process we begin to define our own style and voice.

You may already have an understanding of your natural tendencies in storytelling; if so, wonderful. But if not, let me reassure you that those tendencies are there, that your own voice is waiting, and wanting, to emerge. Finding your voice isn't as simple as finding your car keys, unfortunately—it's a process, again, of trial and error—but a good start might be to try the exercise you'll find in Worksheet 8 on page 241. Write without overthinking what happens, and take note of what patterns you see emerge in your work that might suggest your natural strengths in voice.

TESTING YOUR POV

There's little as frustrating as getting a hundred pages into your novel only to discover you've got some big problems with voice or point of view, so try to make as informed a decision as possible up front. Take a look back at the earlier POV chart and try running your story idea through the questions you find there. When you settle on a possible POV for your novel, test-run it further by asking the questions found in Worksheet 7 on page 240 and making sure it will meet your narrative needs.

BUILDING A WORLD: DESCRIPTION & SETTING

Narration is how you draw your reader into the fictional world you've created. But in order to keep the reader there, you must convince him that the world really exists and is as real as the one he is sitting in. This is accomplished through the use of specific, targeted, and evocative description that engages, and plays upon, the reader's senses. This is the ultimate magic trick of language: to evoke in the reader not just an understanding of the thing described but the sensation of it. It's not enough just to tell a reader the thing exists and ask him to take its existence on faith; you must allow him to experience it for himself.

Just as effective narration has two simultaneous levels of meaning (see page 71), the straight information given to us and a particular way of reading or experiencing that information, effective description not only gives us basic information but evokes a particular feeling about it. For example, giving us the make, model, and color of a car we see on the road is informative—"It was a black '66 Ford Falcon"—but it doesn't necessarily encourage a meaningful response. But when we offer a more evocative description, if we say instead, "It was a big, black, battered, hearselike automobile," a line from Flannery O'Connor's "A Good Man Is Hard to Find," we both visualize the car physically and know how to read it, even out of context: This car looks like Death.

What's more, even though we're all reading the same description, we visualize the car in slightly different ways (for some reason I always put fins on it, like the 1960s Batmobile, and peeling tint on the windows). In my head I know exactly what this death-car looks like, and it's probably different in degree from the way you visualize it. But in spite of the minor variations, we still have a shared experience of what the car means.

Even this brief example illustrates the importance of description and how it functions: In the big picture, it's what allows the author to build the mood, tone, and feel of the fictional world described. But in a smaller sense—and this is the magic act mentioned a moment ago—successful description doesn't force us to accept the author's imagination alone, in some undemocratic way, but engages the reader's imagination, allowing him to participate in the creation of the world. This is why even the most faithful film adaptation of a book we love will never meet our expectations completely; what we see on the screen is how the director visualizes and experiences the fictional world, not the way we did, which is why we leave the theater grumbling about how much the filmmaker got wrong.

Description, then, plays a major role in how well we create believable fiction. So let's take a closer look at what makes description work and how we can use it well.

THE ELEMENTS OF EFFECTIVE DESCRIPTION

Description allows the reader to visualize, understand, and experience the fictional world being described, and it does this by fulfilling certain requirements:

1. Effective description matches up with the voice, tone, and perspective of the narrator. Your narrator has a specific way of looking at and describing the world of your novel, whether it's a first-person narrator or a third person approximating the mind-set of your protagonist. So the first step in crafting description is making sure that you can see through that lens, that your descriptions match up with how your narrator and characters experience the world. Any time we write description that seems not to match up with the voice, tone, and perspective of the narrator, what we're really doing is calling attention to the author instead, reminding a reader she's reading and taking her out of the "reality" of the story.

Take a look at this example from Tim O'Brien's *Going After Cacciato*, about a group of American soldiers, led by protagonist Paul Berlin, who leave their post in Vietnam

On the Subject

Good writing is supposed to evoke sensation in the reader—not the fact that it is raining, but the feeling of being rained upon.
—E.L. Doctorow

(or perhaps have abandoned it) in pursuit of Cacciato, an elusive young private determined to walk from Vietnam to Paris to escape the war. In the following passage, Berlin and his men, having come through the thick marshes and jungles of Vietnam and Laos, begin to encounter the sights, smells, and signs of the more-populated Mandalay. Note how the closeness of the description and its evocation of the senses create this building sense of recognition for both Berlin and for the reader as jungle gives way to city:

> They walked fast along a dirt road that wound through city smells, past rows of mud shanties that soon gave way to concrete tenements. No people yet, but all the signs. Cats and chickens battling in alleyways, gutters with matted trash, a faint hum, the sound of traffic. The road was lined with palmyra and toddy palms. Dogs roamed everywhere: lean and hungry dogs rummaging through garbage, chewing their tails, howling …
>
> … They passed through an arcade that opened into a market square. The place was deserted. They crossed into the bazaar and turned down a cobbled street winding past shops fronted by steel slide-guards. Paul Berlin kept hearing a hum. He couldn't place it but he knew it. No single name, no single sound. A hum.
>
> The streets widened. The garbage smells turned to spice smells. The humming sound suddenly exploded, and he knew its name.
>
> The street became a wide boulevard.
>
> Yellow gas lamps. Fountains spraying colored water. Children romping on trimmed grass, old men on park benches and lovers hand in hand, women pushing baby carriages, people lingering, people chatting and laughing,

bikes and Hondas and carts and buses and donkeys, date trees in neat rows, hedges trimmed and cut square.

"Civilization," Paul Berlin said.

2. Effective description is both surprising and sensible. Description, especially in the forms of metaphor and simile, involves making comparisons between unlike things for the purpose of better visualizing or understanding one of them. This is what figurative language is all about, and when this works well the result is transcendent. Think back to the last image you came across in a novel or short story that struck you with force, a particular way of relating something that caught you by surprise but that also, delivered in this way, made perfect sense, as in the following example from Lorrie Moore's short story "People Like That Are the Only People Here," in which the protagonist, a young mother, notices something strange while changing her baby's diaper:

> A start: the Mother finds a blood clot in the baby's diaper …
> It is big and bright with a broken, khaki-colored vein in it.
> Over the weekend the baby had looked listless and spacey,
> clayey and grim. But today he looks fine—so what is this
> thing, startling against the white diaper, like a tiny mouse
> heart packed in snow?

The visceral, rather straightforward "bright with a broken, khaki-colored vein" and remembrance of the baby's demeanor as "listless and spacey, clayey and grim" show the building horror of this moment very well. But it's this unexpected final image—the clot against the diaper "like a tiny mouse heart packed in snow"—that allows the reader to see this moment clearly and experience the shock for himself.

3. Effective description engages and activates the reader's senses. Visual is obviously the most common form of sensory description, but using all five senses in your work allows your reader an even fuller experience, almost a kind of sympathetic relationship with what's going on in your story. Switching to the underused senses of touch, taste, sound, and smell won't always be required or appropriate, of course—don't tell us what a red brick building tastes like just because you haven't used taste in a while—but when it is called for, the use of these specific sensory details can further the illusion that the world of your novel exists, and that your reader is a part of it.

For a good, quick example, take a look at the following moment from Raymond Carver's "Feathers," the story of a couple who agree to have dinner at the home of one of the man's eccentric coworkers, Bud. From the start, the experience is so bizarre we might be tempted not to believe it—the home contains, among other things, an oddly displayed plaster mold of Bud's wife's malformed teeth; a baby the narrator claims is the ugliest he's ever seen; and a peacock that dive-bombs the narrator's car and later walks around Bud's home freely. But we're made to believe the carnivalesque scene through Carver's sensory description, such as his use of sound:

> I looked around behind Bud and could see that peacock hanging back in the living room, turning its head this way and that, like you'd turn a hand mirror. It shook itself, and the sound was like a deck of cards being shuffled in the other room.

4. Effective description is specific and concrete. I know you know what a headache feels like; everyone's had one, and nobody likes it. So tell me, then: what does a headache feel like? How would you describe one—if I were born without the headache gene, say, or without a head—so that I understand? Can you do it? Likely you'll have to

THE NIGHTTIME NOVELIST

stop thinking about *headache* in general, in the abstract, and try to re-imagine a particularly bad one you once had. Try to remember where it hurt and how, what you noticed in the moment that you wanted desperately to forget, and then begin to channel that description into very specific, particular terms. This is the approach you'll use for all effective description: not to offer some abstract impression of the thing described, assuming that the reader knows enough to fill in the blanks, but to find just the right image that allows us to experience the common thing as if for the first time.

Would you, for example, think to describe woods the way Flannery O'Connor does in one of the tenser moments of "A Good Man is Hard to Find"?: "Behind them the line of woods gaped like a dark open mouth." While we're on the subject, what do snow flurries look like? What about a stagnant body of water? A broken-down car?

In good description there's something both conscious and unconscious going on, beginning with a writer trying to conjure a thing in his imagination and hold it there, channel a new way of seeing or sensing the thing, and then moving into the more conscious deliberation that leads to concrete imagery. This is something non-writers rarely understand—that when you're at a party and suddenly start staring off into nothingness, your eyes glassed over, you're actually doing work—but the process ultimately yields big dividends for you and your reader: A well-wrought image can do more to concretize an object or idea in the mind of your reader than pages of piled-on details ever could.

DESCRIPTION: FIVE CARDINAL SINS

There are two kinds of description that will have your reader waking up his or her spouse to read a line out loud: really good description, and really bad. In order to make sure your descriptions fit in the former category rather than the latter, keep an eye out for the following spouse-elbowing sins of descriptive language and do everything in your power to avoid them.

1. **Mixed metaphors:** A metaphor involves a relationship between two unrelated things, compared in order to better illuminate one of them, as in "The road of life has many sharp turns" (a cliché, true … but we'll take on clichés in just a moment). But when you try to compare one thing to two different things, or try to link one metaphor with another one, what you've got is a mixed metaphor, as in, "The road of life is swimming with dangerous alligators," comparing life to a road and to an alligator pit, I guess. My favorite example of a mixed metaphor comes from Leslie Nielsen as Lt. Frank Drebin in the cinematic masterpiece *The Naked Gun*: "I'm playing hardball, Ludwig. It's fourth and fifteen and you're looking at a full court press."

On the Subject

When you catch an adjective, kill it. No, I don't mean utterly, but kill most of them—then the rest will be valuable.

—*Mark Twain*

2. Other ineffective comparisons: In a metaphor there's a certain relationship: The two things compared must be unrelated, but they can't be incongruous. Thus a metaphor becomes problematic when either (1) the two things compared aren't sufficiently different, or (2) when they're so different the relationship seems nonsensical. An example of the first kind might be simply, "Her tears were streams of water," which makes no sense given that her tears are indeed streams, just not the kind with trout in them. To illustrate the second, where the things compared seem not to match in any way, I turn again to a fictional character, this time George Costanza from *Seinfeld*: "The sea was angry that day, my friends. Like an old man trying to send back soup in a deli."

3. Excessive description: If your handsome, muscular, confident hero strides assertively and briskly into the dusty, spare, barely lamplit room, you've got a problem with excessive description—specifically, with the overuse of adjectives and adverbs. Inexperienced writers are too-often tempted to pile on the modifiers as a shortcut to significant description, though as you see in the example, such piling on is really more distracting than anything else. Some writing teachers will suggest a good rule of thumb is to try to excise adjectives and adverbs from your work altogether, though of course they don't mean this literally. What they mean is, if you're vigilant in keeping control over adjectives and adverbs, the ones that make it in will be there for a reason.

4. Abusing your thesaurus: Does your character imbibe superabundant measures of energizing decoction? Or does he simply drink too much coffee? The simplest, most precise way of saying something is always the best way, whether you're being literal or poetic. (In fact figurative language requires the most precision of all.) So by all means, buy a good thesaurus and stick it on the shelf ... but only reach for it when you're stuck for the best way of saying something and need a nudge. Likewise, there's no reason to have your character strut, stride, amble, jog, or lurch if he can simply walk, nor to have him exhort, exclaim, interrupt, groan, bark, or whine if he can simply say. Using such overdemonstrative verbs when simpler ones would do only makes your character look like a collection of tics rather than a person.

5. Clichés: Clichés are the poetry of the uninspired, a way of making connections and comparisons between unlike things without having to make the effort. But clichés are also insidious, and the thing that makes them insidious is the very thing that makes them clichés in the first place: The more accepted and widely used the cliché, the less likely we are to recognize it as one. We begin to think that the cliché itself has meaning.

Unfortunately, there's no simple rule for spotting clichés in your work; the only way to spot them is to be diligent in searching them out. But once you've found them, there are ways of rehabilitating them, looking at what the clichés are attempting to do and then finding a fresh approach to get at that.

try it out

REIMAGINING CLICHÉS

For more on avoiding and rehabilitating clichés, take a look at Worksheet 9 on page 242 and consider how you might replace the clichéd way of expressing something with a more inspired and direct image.

By the way, you'll notice the last one in the exercise is a bit trickier, as it has to do with conveying emotion through the body, a category of cliché unto itself that includes such dishonorable mentions as *heart pounding, heart soaring, pulse racing, breath getting shallow* or *knees getting weak, shiver going up your spine, chest swelling with pride, head throbbing*, and so on. These are among the most insidious clichés of all, because we tend to believe them accurate (but my stomach really did drop!). Nevertheless, approach these as you would any other cliché you come across: by finding a new way to express the idea so we experience the emotion right along with the character.

CRAFTING YOUR SETTING (AND WHY IT MATTERS)

Every time we do something as simple as put an adjective and noun together, what we've begun to do is create a world. Now granted, depending upon your aims in fiction and the needs of the story you're trying to tell, the world you create might end up bearing a striking resemblance to the one in which we live. But the truth is that every novelist—from the historical to the speculative to the writer interested in exploring the here and now—builds her fictional world in the same way, rendering it through precise detail according to the tonal, thematic, and logistical requirements of story and character.

To put it another way, setting—the time, place, and space of your story—isn't simply four walls you've dropped your character into so he'll have someplace to sit, nor is it a larger, objective, impersonal world that only just happens to include the people you're focusing on, tangentially. Setting is directly related to your character, another way of revealing and deepening our understanding of him and his quest. In this way, setting serves a kind of double function: How your character relates to his environment tells us, on a practical

On the Subject

I always try to make the setting fit the story I have in mind.

—Tony Hillerman

level, something about the environment, allowing us to visualize the world alongside your protagonist—and hopefully to experience it in a similar way—but the character's relationship to his environment also tells us something about the character himself. You might think of your fictional world as a hall of mirrors; everything your character sees and experiences offers a reflection of him.

Let's consider a hypothetical example: Say your main character is a struggling musician who works a day job he hates and plays dive bars around town at night trying to get noticed. So now that we have the basics we need—a protagonist with a clear motivation and two settings—how would we describe these settings to match up with the protagonist, given what we know about him?

Well, the office would be described in ways that show everything he dislikes (despises) about working there, about that life—the fake-white light, the kind of bright, soulless light under which autopsies are performed; the cramped cubicles practically piled on top of one another, barely big enough to fit your elbows inside, the dividers so thin every phone conversation is a shared experience; the plastic clacking of keyboards; the forced, unfunny laughter of an e-mail forward received three cubicles down … .

How about the dive bars, our second major setting? How might they be described? Naturally, it depends on the character's feelings about them (and maybe whether we intend on allowing him to meet his goal). If we're telling a hopeful story, then these nighttime bars might look like freedom itself, like the antithesis of the restriction of the office workplace—the bar lights down and comfortably dim, the random laughter from the darkness broken but real, the place giving off a kind of music of its own, the percussion of beer mugs clinked in celebration of nothing in particular and the pop of billiards from a back corner table, the protagonist's awkward breathing into the mic, coughing and clearing his throat, then that first hesitant chord … .

But what if these dive bars are a disaster? What if, instead of a place humming with life, these bars are depressed versions of the local VFW, a crowd of four old guys drinking at the bar, all of them alone, and a plump bartender with a rose tattoo on her cleavage, which she covers by crossing her arms over her breasts and staring disinterestedly toward the stage as our protagonist struggles to get that B string in tune … in tuuuuuune … in tuuuuuuuuuu-uuune … ?

Even these quickly sketched places illustrate how setting and character reflect one another, become aspects of the same thing, and this will be the case every time you shift to a new setting in your novel, with each new place and environment revealing something about your protagonist. It might be helpful to think of settings as major and minor: the major settings—those places you'll come to, and perhaps return to, at key points in your character or plot arc—tend to reflect big-picture aspects of character, motivation, and conflict (in the example of the struggling musician, both the office and the dive bars seem to be major settings, not only places we'll spend a good bit of time in but places that are directly meaningful in the character's quest). The minor settings we might use could speak to the character's overall arc, or they may simply speak to the arc of a particular scene: what the character wants in the moment, and what's currently standing in his way.

Thus, a music store the protagonist frequents—for strings, maybe, or to strum a guitar he can't afford—might speak to the overall character arc if the shaggy clerk behind the counter is a version of him, or perhaps a version of his deeper fears (for example, the clerk is a "frontman" for a "band" that hasn't had a gig or even a practice in five years, a testament to the reality of failure, or maybe the unreality of not realizing the dream is dead, dude). Or the music store might have a smaller arc of its own, a subplot: the shaggy burnout clerk always spots the protagonist and follows him around the store, incessantly rambling, when our protagonist has only ten minutes on his lunch break to grab his strings and get back to the office. How you use description to bring each setting to life depends on the character's view of the place and what the place means for you in telling the story. And once you've begun thinking of setting in these terms, you'll know what sorts of specific details to bring out to make your settings meaningful and real.

Think about your major settings first, starting with the places your protagonist will find himself the most, then think about what the places really mean to him, how the character feels about, or in, those places, how they reflect some part of him and his arc. Once you have an idea of the character's relationship to the place, think of what specific details you might emphasize to show that relationship and allow the reader to experience the place in the same way.

MAJOR & MINOR SETTINGS

Begin thinking about your major and minor settings—and how these will match up or help show your protagonist and his quest—by looking at Worksheet 11: Crafting a Setting and Worksheet 12: Major & Minor Settings on pages 245 and 246. It might also be helpful to look back at the earlier worksheet on description to see how your work there might suggest how to go about conveying setting; again, both description and setting come to the reader filtered through POV and voice—what's said and how it's said—which themselves mirror and reveal plot, character, conflict, and so on.

Thus, as you brainstorm from worksheet to worksheet, building one to the next, you should begin to see consistent patterns, repeated images, and larger tone suggested. Think about the ways your major and minor settings can help reflect and reveal what you've already established with character and story. (Worksheet 11 is an exercise designed to get you thinking of setting in ways particular to your character and his relationship to a given place.)

PUTTING IT ALL TOGETHER

We've spent a good bit of time pulling fiction apart, considering its components and how they work. Now, as we turn our attention toward novel-writing proper, it's important to remind ourselves something I'm sure we already know: When fiction works, the individual components become difficult to parse out and separate from one another, become a unified experience that leads the reader not to quibble with, or even to recognize, the individual components but to accept the fictional world as complete. Plot, character, conflict, voice, description, setting, word-by-word storytelling … all of this is really about how to hide the card up your sleeve, how to palm the quarter, how to make sure the rabbit we've chosen fits into the top hat. But the reader doesn't want to see how the trick is done. The reader wants a magic act.

By this point we could take a look at a piece of fiction and see how and why it works, see how the individual parts create a cohesive and compelling whole, and this is a useful exercise to do throughout the writing, if for no other reason than to remind us of how effortless all of this actually seems when it's done well. But the only way we'll know for sure that our own apprenticeship is done, that we've learned what we need to, is to step out on stage ourselves.

OPENING SCENE & FIRST-ACT STRUCTURE

The beginning of your novel is the moment in which your fictional world, which has taken on an abstract shape in your head, comes into concrete existence ... and immediately has a lot to accomplish. Your opening scene introduces the reader to the world and grounds him in it; introduces the protagonist and lets the reader inside his heart and head, showing us why we should care about him; reveals what's at stake for him and what stands in his way; and both suggests to the reader what's still to come and leaves enough mystery so that the reader isn't sure what will come, and has to keep reading to find out.

If this sounds like a lot, don't worry: You've already begun your novel in the right way, starting with a clear understanding of character, motivation, and conflict and considering how everything else aligns with these. You found a narrative approach, in your POV and voice, that works for your story. You've already considered the larger arc of your novel, and you did some test-runs of your narrative choices to make sure they'll be able to propel your arc forward. You've considered how your descriptions and settings align with and help reveal your protagonist and his journey. All of this is important, and the care and thoughtfulness you've shown should make you feel confident heading in.

Nevertheless, the ultimate test of your story and approach really comes now, as you craft opening lines and scenes that should not only allow you to tell your story the way you want to, and keep your reader interested and engaged, but that also keep *you* interested and engaged, making you excited to discover what happens next as you move from line to line.

COMPONENTS OF A GOOD OPENING SCENE

In *The First Five Pages: A Writer's Guide to Staying Out of the Rejection Pile*, writer and former literary agent Noah Lukeman claims that the amount of time you have to grab your reader's attention—including that of an agent or editor—is, you guessed it, five pages. Lukeman may've been a bit generous in this; other testimonies I've heard put the number closer to one page. Or half of one.

Whatever the actual number, and no matter how intimidating it ends up being, the message is undeniable: Your story has to start with a strong opening scene. And despite the fact that all of us will be writing very different novels, on varied subjects and in divergent styles, there are a number of components that all good opening scenes have in common.

A good opening scene:

1. Has a compelling hook. A hook is an opening line that entices the reader into your story by (1) beginning in a clear moment of action or interaction and (2) serving as a tease, revealing just enough information to ground the reader in

On the Subject

The value of a well-written opening is that it makes the reader ready to give himself to the writer's imagined people for the duration.

—*Sol Stein*

the moment while maintaining enough mystery—through the careful omission of certain information—to keep her reading.

By moment of action, I don't mean that you begin with a bomb ticking, or someone running for his life, or a massive explosion. Rather it means that you avoid synopsis, stage direction, and backstory by dropping us directly into a scene in progress so that we're in the midst of the action, or *in medias res*. (Such a direct opening can be particularly difficult for the meticulous writer, who's thought so much about her protagonist and his backstory that she's not really sure where to begin.)

Likewise, the tease of a compelling hook is not about intentionally hiding things from the reader, making it difficult for her to figure out what's going on. Inexperienced writers often confuse abstraction for mystery, and they'll believe that an interesting opening scene is one where the reader has no clue what's going on and has to figure it out for himself, as when the reader is dropped into the middle of a dream, or a drug trip, or a riot, or the ocean, or whatever. ("What was that? Who's talki—wait, something was touching her now—Is that a voice she heard? Who's talking? And what was touching her on the leg? And is that a white glowing mist in the distance—?") The result, as you can see, is less one of mystery than frustration, which is obviously not what you want your reader to experience—on page one or anywhere else.

So let's consider what we do mean by a compelling hook. Let's say your opening scene takes place in a dentist's office, with your protagonist going in for a root canal. Probably your first inclination would be to begin with some straight-up information getting the character there: "Barbara Morris walked into the dentist's office and up to the receptionist's window to sign in for her root canal." But while that's very informative, it's also a bit of a bore. How, then, might we convey the same basic information—we're in a dentist's office for a procedure—that begins in the action of the moment and also holds enough mystery to convince the reader to keep going?

Maybe something like this: "Barbara Morris breathed in the hissing gas and immediately felt her face sliding off her skull."

At the baseline, this conveys the same basic information as the previous first line we tried. But it puts us in the moment, with the reader feeling as if he has that little hissing mask on his face, too, already an improvement over the first. Plus, in the first line we tried out, there's very little mystery involved; we know what's likely to come next (the character is going to speak to the receptionist). But in the second one, we get the feeling that anything might still happen: Barbara Morris might panic and try to take the mask off; she might accidentally reveal her darkest secret while loopy on gas; she might look at those two hairy dentist's hands coming toward her and suddenly realize she's in love. We don't know what'll happen next, but hopefully we're intrigued enough to read to the next line to find out.

And all of this is accomplished by starting with something fairly general (going to the dentist), considering what exact moment there we might focus on to begin, and finding a first line that conveys the moment in an interesting way and makes us, as authors, want to *write* the next line.

2. Grounds us in the protagonist's perspective. It's good to begin in a moment of action or interaction, something to grab the reader's attention right away, but it's important to remember that your reader experiences your fictional world as your protagonist does. Thus a good opening scene is one that grounds us in the main character's perspective, shows us the world through his eyes, from the very beginning.

Immediate action that's not grounded in character is just Stuff Happening and can be disorienting for a reader. As an editor and teacher I see this quite a bit: stories that begin with a gun battle, for instance, with characters barking out orders and bullets flying and lots of Stuff Happening—high action, the author thinks, this'll hook a reader—but that offers no way for the reader to know whom to root for, whom to run from, what's important and what's just chaos. And our reaction to such a scene at the beginning of a novel is much the same as if we'd been dropped into a gun battle in real life: Get me outta here.

This is the double burden of a solid opening: introduce the character and get us into his head and heart while simultaneously engaging us in action. But when you find that opening that does both of these things well, the chances are good that your reader—not to mention your potential editor and publisher—will be drawn into the story and will feel compelled to keep going.

NOTE: The use of the third-person omniscient narrator for a novel with a large cast (e.g. the example on pages 75–6 from Susanna Clarke's *Jonathan Strange & Mr. Norrell*) might seem like a possible exception to the "protagonist first" rule, but if you go back and take a look at those introductory lines, you'll see that we're still grounded by a particular perspective and personality from the start: that of the omniscient-narrator-as-storyteller.

3. Has a complete arc of its own but also urges us toward the next. Your opening scene has an arc of its own: We have our protagonist, who we understand has a clear internal motivation because we're grounded in the protagonist's perspective; we have a conflict, which comes up against the character's motivation or want; and finally we have a resolution that's satisfying by the scene's end—though the way the arc plays out should raise a number of related questions that keep us reading, to see how those questions or problems play out.

It's tempting to think of your opening scene as an introduction, something that's slyly moving pieces into place that'll become revelatory later, and in a sense this is what an opening scene does (as we'll discuss in just a moment). But your first scene can't merely be a scene that delays, that promises something more important coming later on if you'll just keep reading; we need to see stakes right away. Making sure your scene has a complete arc is one way you assure the reader has a sense of something at stake immediately, even if what's at risk in this first scene is relatively minor in relation to what's coming up (as you get to the first act's Inciting Incident and Plot Point 1 that leads us to the second act, both of which raise the overall stakes even more).

But while the arc we see play out in the opening scene must be, in relation to what's coming up, minor, your opening scene can't simply be a throwaway scene, just a quick conflict for conflict's sake; in fact, this first minor arc and how it plays out will resonate throughout the rest of your book. And that's because a good opening scene …

4. Contains or suggests the end of your novel. What's that? We have to start thinking about the end so soon? Actually, yes. There are really two closely related arcs launched at the beginning of your novel: one that plays out and resolves itself by the end of the opening scene (the external motivation and conflict of the particular moment), and one that plays out over the course of the book (the character's internal motivation and conflict: what's revealed about what he wants in the longer run). Thus, an important consideration in crafting your opening scene is to begin thinking about and crafting the end of your novel, planning for how you believe the story will resolve, and then making sure that whatever ending or resolution you have in mind is established in the beginning.

Think back, for example, to the overall arc of *The Wizard of Oz*. We begin and end that story in the same place, Kansas—I defy you not see it in black-and-white—though the scenes we have in the beginning and end are poles apart from each other, showing the far ends of Dorothy's arc. In the beginning we see Dorothy feeling unwanted and unsure she belongs, wishing she were someplace else; at the end, we see her knowing that this is home, the place she belongs. That ending scene is the completion of what we see of Dorothy's arc from the very first scene. In the beginning of that story is the end.

HOW AN EFFECTIVE OPENING SETS THE STAKES

Let's look at an example of a good opening scene and see how everything syncs up, using the beginning of Stephen King's *The Shining* as an example. (If you have a copy sitting on your bookshelf, you might want to pull it down and reread the opening chapter to play along at home.)

First, let's note how much work King manages right up front, with his very first line:

> Jack Torrance thought: Officious little prick.

This is a clear, effective hook: We know there's a character named Jack Torrance, and we know somebody else in the room is, apparently, an officious little prick, though we don't know who, or why, or if he really is—until we keep reading. The line begins in thought, in Torrance's head (via the third-person narrator), but you'll note that the line is still active, beginning by revealing interaction between two characters, Torrance and the officious little prick, though we haven't seen them interact yet.

On the Subject

One of the most difficult things is the first paragraph. I have spent many months on a first paragraph and once I get it, the rest comes out very easily. In the first paragraph you solve most of the problems with your book. The theme is defined, the style, the tone.

—*Gabriel Garcia Marquez*

Secondly, this line grounds us in the protagonist's perspective. We know exactly how Torrance feels about whoever is in the room with him, and we see that person through Jack's eyes. If there's anything that throws us off, it's the seething anger coming from our protagonist, which is something that's necessary for King to establish. But I'm getting ahead of myself ...

Third, the line establishes its own arc, a conflict between our protagonist and the unnamed antagonist. And we don't have to wait long to get more details about the conflict:

> Ullman stood five-five, and when he moved, it was with the prissy speed that seems to be the exclusive domain of all small plump men. The part in his hair was exact, and his dark suit was sober but comforting. I am a man you can bring your problems to, that suit said to the paying customer. To the hired help it spoke more curtly: This had better be good, you. There was a red carnation in the lapel, perhaps so that no one on the street would mistake Stuart Ullman for the local undertaker.
>
> As he listened to Ullman speak, Jack admitted to himself that he probably could not have liked any man on that side of the desk—under the circumstances.
>
> Ullman had asked a question he hadn't caught. That was bad; Ullman was the type of man who would file such lapses away in a mental Rolodex for later consideration.
>
> "I'm sorry?"
>
> "I asked if your wife fully understood what you would be taking on here. And there's your son, of course." He glanced down at the application in front of him. "Daniel. Your wife isn't a bit intimidated by the idea?"

So the situation, and the scene's arc, is a job interview. The external motivation in the scene? Jack Torrence wants a job as the winter caretaker of the Overlook Hotel, an isolated, claustrophobic place completely shut off from the outside world at the first snowfall, home to a tragic past and epically bad juju … nice work if you can get it, I guess. The external conflict, the thing standing in Jack's way, is Ullman, the guy with the power and the clipboard. This is an easy enough arc for a first scene, and it'll resolve in one of two ways: Jack will get the position or he won't.

What about internal motivation? What does this rather simple arc reveal about Jack as a person that we'll see play out throughout the book?

Officious little prick.

Jack Torrance really needs this job. He and his family have fallen on hard times (more in a moment) and Jack sees this as an opportunity to do something positive, turn his and his family's lives around. Nevertheless, Jack doesn't really behave in the scene like a man begging for a job, does he? Do we see him acting humble, or agreeable, or enthusiastic? Think back to the last job you really wanted and how you behaved and even *thought* while in the interview. Were you putting your best self forward, agreeable to a fault? Trying your best to smile on the inside as well as out?

Jack's anger is a bit bizarre considering what he's here to do. In fact, in the fourth paragraph Jack is so caught up in mentally berating Ullman that he actually misses a question Ullman asks him. And as the scene goes on, Jack's thoughts are constantly interrupted by the same kind of bile:

> Jack's hands were clenched tightly in his lap, working against each other, sweating. Officious little prick, officious little prick, officious—

Jack Torrance, to put it mildly, has a bit of an anger problem. And Ullman is aware of this, aware that Jack's previous job, teaching English at a prep school, ended abruptly over an "incident." Oh yes, Jack has also

THE NIGHTTIME NOVELIST

had a problem with the booze. Ullman doesn't think Jack is right for the demanding job and has reservations: The hotel has had a history of caretakers breaking down and going nuts, a result of the isolation, such as happened with the late Delbert Grady, who killed his family with a hatchet before turning a shotgun on himself. When Jack smiles his big PR smile and tells Ullman he has nothing whatsoever to worry about, we know that we, as readers, certainly do. The smaller arc of the scene is finished when Ullman gives Jack the job, but the larger arc that comes from Jack's internal motivation and conflict—his wanting to be a better man and take care of his family vs. his occasional blinding rage—is one we'll watch play out to the very end. Though occasionally we'll watch through barely parted fingers.

For more on how King manages all of this in his first chapter, take a look at the book itself ... or pull another off the shelf that you admire and consider how that author manages the opening scene. Then do a little planning, going through the steps with your own story idea, seeing how your opening scene might accomplish what it needs to.

When the planning is done, there's one thing left: Write your opening scene.

A CHECKLIST OF CLICHÉD OR INEFFECTIVE OPENINGS

If agent Noah Lukeman is right, and the first five pages are of vital importance to the overall success of your novel, then you want to make absolutely sure there's nothing in those pages which might turn a reader, or an editor, away. The best way to do that is to make sure your opening meets the conditions discussed in the previous section, but you also want to make sure you avoid some common problems and insidious clichés of novel beginnings that could land your book in the trash quickly.

Specifically, you must do everything in your power to avoid the following:

1. Beginning in abstraction. We already discussed this in the previous section, but it bears repeating: You don't want to begin your novel in any kind of elusive or illusory quagmire where the reader doesn't understand, right from the start, what's going on or where he is. Abstraction, as I said before, is not the same thing as mystery, so you'll want to avoid the following, any of which might be disorienting for the reader:

- Beginning in a dream, fantasy, drug haze, hallucination, or virtual reality

- Dropping the reader into a gunfight, chase scene, natural disaster, riot, or other scene of instantaneous mass confusion

- Dropping the reader into a dialogue between two or more unidentified, not-immediately-named people

- Beginning with summary, lecture, philosophizing, or any other litany

- Beginning in a foreign (or alien) language (or, for that matter, in any language that's not clear to comprehend)

2. Beginning in cliché. It may've indeed been a dark and stormy night, but you sure can't start off saying that it was. A cliché that shows up on your first page tells your reader one thing: that every page that follows is filled with clichés, too. Look out especially for the following:

- Beginning with a ringing phone, alarm clock, or doorbell (Dishonorable mention: ominous church bells where everyone in a village looks up simultaneously, then shuffles indoors fast. If the bells ring at the same time every day—presumably once an hour, too, right?—then why does it always catch you nervous peasants by surprise?)

- Beginning with a character waking up with a start, as if from a nightmare caused by bad late-night food

- Beginning with a literally ticking clock or bomb

- Beginning with clichéd language and images (*She had legs that just wouldn't quit.* Well, the reader knows how to make them quit. Just close the book.)

3. Beginning in melodrama or heightened emotion. Dropping the reader into a scene of already heightened emotion, when we have no idea who the characters involved are, is like watching a couple having a fight in public: We know someone's having an emotional reaction, but the only thing we really feel is embarrassed (and like backing away). Don't simply display that emotion up front—no matter the emotion you're going for— but find a way to lead the reader into the story so that we experience the emotion for ourselves. Along those lines, be careful of the following:

- Beginning in a moment of physical or verbal altercation (This only matters to us if we know what it's about, who's involved, how to feel about it, and so on.)

- Beginning with a sex scene (A little intimate for an introduction, right?)

- Beginning with a phone call delivering tragic news

- Beginning in any heightened emotion that doesn't have a clear character to whom we can ascribe the emotion and begin to understand it

A few things I'd like to point out: First, this is an imperfect, incomplete list. The only way to really catch any problematic or clichéd opening is to be on the lookout for it (and, perhaps, to have a reader you trust take a look and offer advice). Second, even the openings on this list are, to some degree, negotiable. If you really *need* to open your novel with a ringing phone, you can hopefully find some new and compelling way of doing so, so long as you're aware of the potential risks involved and can find a way to do it that doesn't feel hackneyed. For an example I offer the beginning of Paul Auster's postmodern refiguring of the detective story, *City of Glass*:

> It was a wrong number that started it, the telephone ringing
> three times in the dead of night, and the voice on the other

end asking for someone he was not. Much later, when he was able to think about the things that happened to him, he would conclude that nothing was real except chance. But that was much later.

True, part of what Auster is doing in *City of Glass* is consciously playing on the clichés and tropes of detective fiction, exploiting them for his own purposes, but this is nevertheless a fine example of an author remaking a clichéd opening so that it becomes interesting again—here by minimizing the clanging bringbring and adding mystery through this teasing narrative voice and its use of time, the "much later" that piques our interest.

Which brings us to one last point: to a certain degree all ideas are unoriginal and run the risk of cliché; it's our *approach* that makes the familiar seem fresh and new. However you begin your novel, take pains to see that your approach is truly novel—something that attracts and then urges the reader to move forward.

THE SHAPE OF THE FIRST ACT

In conventional three-act structure, the first act accounts for roughly 25 percent of the story—for a 250-page novel, the first fifty pages, or thereabouts—and accomplishes the following:

- Introduces the protagonist and her internal motivation in the Setup (the first act also introduces the main external motivation, sometimes at the same moment as the internal or sometimes thereafter but never before, as we need to know who the character is to know why, or if, we care)

- Uses an early Inciting Incident to introduce conflict in order to illustrate what's at stake for the character in her quest and what will stand in her way

- Ends on the first major Plot Point, a pivotal moment that propels us and the character into a new, but related, direction, launching the second act (and the story proper, as we probably think of it)

These terms can often be a bit confusing on their own—it helps to look at them in action, as we'll do momentarily—but just to say a word about them: the Setup is easy enough to see, introducing the character and her internal motivation, who she is and what she values (which will be significant for the rest of the book when what she values or wants is continually put at risk). The first time her internal motivation is at risk is in the Inciting Incident, which is not yet the major conflict in the story—that comes at

Plot Point 1, the turning point into the second act—but which, nevertheless, suggests the personal stakes. Think of the Inciting Incident as a minor version, a foreshadowing, of the larger conflict to come. Now, there's no set format or time span for these first-act moments to come about; they might be spread out over the course of the act, or they may come more or less at once. The important thing to note, however, is that these are incremental, beginning with showing us who the character is at heart, then suggesting what the stakes are for her personally before introducing the bigger conflict that puts her wants and goals in peril. No matter where the points come in the first act, this is the proper order for our character, and our understanding of the stakes, to build.

The last bullet point above also deserves a moment's attention: When we think of *The Wizard of Oz*, what do we think of? Most likely, Dorothy in Oz. When we think of *The Silence of the Lambs*, we think of Clarice Starling tracking down the serial killer Buffalo Bill and racing the clock. *Lord of the Rings?* Frodo and company traveling to Mordor and trying to avoid any number of conflicts along the way.

In all of the above examples what comes to mind first is the *second* act, the events that comprise the bulk of the story. What the first act does, then, is set up what's important about the character and situation so that we have a clear understanding of what's at stake throughout the second act ... which we won't see resolved, of course, until the big finale in the third act. But even if the first act gets less attention than the two that follow, the success of the final two is dependent upon how well we set up the story in the first. Without Kansas up front, Oz just isn't the same place.

Let's run our aforementioned three examples through the requirements of a first act and make sure we understand its scope and shape:

THE WIZARD OF OZ

Opening Scene and Setup	Inciting Incident	Plot Point 1
introduces character and motivation	conflict which reveals personal stakes for the protagonist	turning point which changes the dynamic of the story and launches Act II
Orphaned Dorothy lives on a farm with her aunt and uncle, who seem not to understand her. They pay little attention to her, and the only real companion she has is her dog Toto. Dorothy doesn't fit in, even though this is "home." The book makes the point clear, as does the film, by describing not just the aunt and uncle but the house and countryside as "gray" and humorless; Dorothy is the lively girl stuck in the middle of a seemingly dead, foreign place. Dorothy wants to fit in on the farm, though the book tells us that, of everything there, only Toto "was not gray; he was a little black dog." Dorothy wants simply to feel loved and accepted... though the only way she finds this acceptance, at the beginning of the book, is through Toto, not her preoccupied aunt and uncle and the help.	Almira Gulch, the mean townswoman bitten by Toto, threatens to have Toto taken and destroyed. She even brings a sheriff who takes the dog, though Toto escapes. Thus the only family Dorothy has that's close to her, who seems to love her unconditionally, has been threatened ... and Dorothy's aunt and uncle seem unconcerned with helping her, furthering her feelings of isolation. NOTE: This Inciting Incident comes from the film version rather than the novel; the book gets us to Oz much more quickly, and in a less psychologically desperate way. (No threatening to euthanize a dog in the book.)	The twister, which picks up the Gale house, and Dorothy and Toto along with it, and lands them in Oz. The moment Dorothy opens the door and steps into Oz, we're in Act II. (Again, the shape of this closely mirrors the film; we arrive in Oz in the book at the beginning of chapter 2.)

THE SILENCE OF THE LAMBS

Opening Scene and Setup	Inciting Incident	Plot Point 1
introduces character and motivation	conflict which reveals personal stakes for the protagonist	turning point which changes the dynamic of the story and launches Act II
Clarice Starling is called into Jack Crawford's office and asked to help with the Buffalo Bill case by interviewing Dr. Hannibal Lecter. This opening scene is a version of getting called into the principal's office, though it ends not with a reprimand but an opportunity. Starling agrees to visit Lecter and try to do as Crawford asks, to help with the case; she wants to seize an opportunity and show she's up to the larger personal task of proving herself and making a life and career for herself. It even leads her to accept an assignment that's perhaps over her head, though she might not realize yet how far over her head she is.	Starling meets with Lecter, who toys with her mind— "like an alien consciousness loose in her head," the text tells us—and then rebuffs her, but not before yielding a clue on a person named Raspil. The Lecter moments in the first part of the book show us what's at stake in the Buffalo Bill case, what it is the FBI is dealing with ... but more importantly what's increasingly at stake for Starling personally, as Lecter develops an interest in stripping her down and exploring her psyche and motivations.	Catherine Martin, daughter of Senator Ruth Martin, becomes the latest woman kidnapped by Buffalo Bill, automatically raising the stakes and sense of urgency with the investigation (and the novel). Starling makes a deal with Lecter to help save Catherine Martin before she's killed. This is the turning point and changes the dynamic, launching Act II ... a transition made even clearer in the film version, when Anthony Hopkins looks into the camera and says plainly, "I'll help you catch him, Clarice." And the audience goes, "Ooooooo ..."

THE LORD OF THE RINGS: THE FELLOWSHIP OF THE RING

Opening Scene and Setup	Inciting Incident	Plot Point 1
introduces character and motivation	conflict which reveals personal stakes for the protagonist	turning point which changes the dynamic of the story and launches Act II
The town of Hobbiton throws a party for Bilbo Baggins on his eleventy-first birthday. (Bilbo's advanced age is already a clue to what's to come, a result of his possessing the One Ring for many years.) *LOTR* is obviously epic in scale, concerning Frodo as a protagonist, yes, but also having a much bigger cast of characters and implications for everyone in Middle Earth, not just the protagonist. Thus, while we're introduced to Frodo early on, what we're really shown as a motivation in the opening scenes and set-up is this world itself, this way of life, which will soon be threatened.	At his birthday party, Bilbo makes an odd speech, a goodbye speech, which ends with his slipping the One Ring onto his finger and disappearing. This is the first indication Frodo—or anyone else—has that there is something bigger going on than just a birthday party ... the first disruption of the Hobbits' idyllic way of life, but not the last. More, Bilbo's slipping on the One Ring alerts Sauron—the antagonist who wants possession of it—that the Ring has been found and is in someone's possession. That's enough to show that the Shire and its way of life are now at risk.	The wizard Gandalf gives the One Ring to Bilbo's nephew Frodo—Gandalf doesn't want to be tempted by its power—and tells Frodo to leave the Shire with it; Gandalf will meet with Frodo at the Prancing Pony, an inn, where they will regroup. Frodo's leaving the Shire marks the beginning of a long second act spent on the move. But it's also the beginning of a much longer journey—one that won't fully be done until Frodo takes the Ring back to Mordor to destroy it, at the end of the third book in the trilogy, *The Return of the King*.

THE NIGHTTIME NOVELIST

If you judged from this information alone, you might think that the first acts of all three stories have only three things happen in them ... which is, of course, not the case. Instead the space between the opening, Inciting Incident, and Plot Point 1 is filled in different ways, according to the needs of the authors and the particular stories: *The Silence of the Lambs*, which operates as a mystery or detective story, sees Agent Starling finding and following leads, the pursuit of which sometimes leads her back to Lecter, sometimes back to her mentor Jack Crawford, and sometimes out into the world. Because she's a trainee, we also have scenes that show her student life and difficulties in juggling responsibilities; because she's studying forensics, we have a scene where she helps perform an autopsy, etc. It's not as if Harris is simply stalling between the opening and later pivotal moments; rather, Starling's particular situation and who she is—not to mention the expectations that come in telling a mystery/detective story—lend themselves to a number of potential choices in the storytelling. Following those choices, watching them play out, allows Harris to lead naturally through the act, up to and past the Inciting Incident with Lecter and leading finally to the abduction of Catherine Martin, which changes the game for all involved.

The Lord of the Rings: The Fellowship of the Ring, on the other hand, is obviously a very different type of novel, and thus Tolkien follows different lines of storytelling between the opening, Inciting Incident, and first Plot Point: We have slower-paced scenes of Hobbit life and carousing; moments of song, dance, and poetry; lively dialogue and description; and, because Tolkien uses a third-person omniscient "storytelling" narrator, moments of background and perspective that take their time in creating the almost fairy-tale atmosphere of the book. In other words, Tolkien has in mind the Inciting Incident and first Plot Point and knows what they will be, just as Harris does, but his getting there is quite different from Harris's, particular to the kind of story he's telling.

You should consider the shape of your own first act the same way: You know where the story starts, and you'll have an idea of the key scenes coming up that will serve as the Inciting Incident and Plot Point 1. It's absolutely not necessary, by the way, that you think of these moments in these terms, stressing out about having an "Inciting Incident." You might just as easily think of these as major and minor "turning points" you'll get to, and you probably wouldn't lose anything to do so. Inciting Incident and Plot Point 1 are just names of markers, moments that you know are important and will occur at crucial intervals in the first act. But how and when you arrive at those markers depends upon what you want to do in your storytelling ... including what happens in the telling you maybe didn't anticipate.

Within the framework of knowing where your first act begins and ends, you have to allow for moments when you are pleasantly surprised by the direction the narrative takes. Begin by crafting your opening scene, as we discussed earlier, and when you finish writing the scene, see if a second scene is suggested by how you left off in the first. Be on the lookout as you go for secondary characters who seem to take on lives of their own and who you might want to revisit later as a subplot. Don't think too far ahead of where you're writing (don't constantly tell yourself, in other words, "I need to be at the Inciting Incident in X more pages!!"). Write your novel one scene at a time, making sure that each one has its own arc, its own purpose and life, while also suggesting where to go next. If you approach the work this way, your novel should begin to find its forward momentum so that without overplanning you find yourself writing toward the Inciting Incident you had in mind all along, and shortly thereafter toward Plot Point 1. Make sure you keep your pacing tight throughout—take a look at Pacing: How to Keep Your Plot (and Reader) Moving Forward on page 147 if you feel a particular section has begun to wander or drag—but also be open to where the story takes you and how the characters begin directing you.

In short, the beginning of your novel requires this almost zen-like balance of freedom and control, of knowing what major plot and character moments to hit (and when the right time is to hit them) while also embracing unanticipated directions and line-by-line surprise. Too much rigid control reads like pure sweat and toil; too much freedom seems haphazard and sloppy. But the right balance feels alive and encourages the reader to keep turning pages, the same way it encourages you to keep writing them.

FIRST-ACT FRAMEWORK

Back in Shaping the Novel: Three-Act Structure, we discussed novel structure as managing both the macro and micro. Establishing those pivotal moments and markers to write toward in the first act is important in keeping your overall plot shapely and forward-moving. To that end, take a look at Worksheet 13: First-Act Markers and Worksheet 14: Setup & Opening Scene Sketch on pages 247 and 248, respectively, and consider those pivotal moments for your own first act.

But you should keep in mind that the ultimate goal of making a first-act framework isn't to confine you but just the opposite: Establishing a framework actually frees you up to focus on the micro and the moment-by-moment. So don't feel restricted by what's ahead of you; don't spend your writing time always worried with what's coming next. Rather, start out where your book starts out—with a compelling opening scene—and give the scene what it needs, looking back to the beginning of this section, if you need, for a reminder of how an opening scene operates and what it does. Focus your attention on making this scene everything it needs to be to hook the reader. Then, when you've finished the scene, consider what the natural next scene might be, hit return a few times (or open a new document if you're beginning a brand new chapter) and give the same attention to this scene, beginning with an interesting hook, introducing conflict and watching how your character deals with it, and allowing the voice you've set up to tell the story and lead you along, naturally (and organically) leading toward the big-picture moments you've got in mind.

Above all, you should keep in mind that writing, while often demanding work, is high-level play. You're creating a reality that never existed until you said so. Don't forget to enjoy yourself along the way.

PART ONE
COFFEE BREAK

PLANNING FOR YOUR MIDDLE

In the beginning of your book, you set up what your main character wants and suggest what's at stake for him if he fails. In the middle, or the second act, the suggestion stops and the stakes become much more real. The second act is really the *heart* of your book, the section in which your protagonist's abilities and re-solve are put to the test and his goal is most at risk. It's also the part of the book most consider the story proper—Ahab chasing the whale, Dorothy navigating Oz—and it likely contains those key moments of action or conflict you've really been itching to write since you first began brainstorming your story.

As you move into your own second act, here are some questions you should consider:

What kinds of conflict will stand in my protagonist's way? A club to the back of the head seems a pretty obvious obstacle to overcome, but keep in mind that subtler, quieter conflicts can be just as perilous, as long as they directly threaten your hero's quest. Think about how your character might come into not just physical conflict but personal conflict, professional conflict, psychological conflict, even moral conflict ... whatever logically might stand in the way of his goal (and make the reader bite her fingernails a bit).

What is your protagonist willing to do to achieve his goal? How far would he be willing to go? Would he toe the line morally or ethically, or sneak a toe across if he had to? For that matter, given how important the goal is to him and why—as the reader understands from the setup in the first act—would the protagonist cross the line altogether? As the conflict becomes direr, and the quest more imperiled, your protagonist will be tested in exactly this way—addressing not just what he is able to do, practically speaking, but what he is *capable* of, as a person.

What would happen if the protagonist failed in his quest? Your second act will begin to answer this question, as each new conflict faced increases the likelihood—and the reader's anxiety—that the hero *might* fail.

Let's move on to the second act ... and find out what your protagonist is made of.

PART TWO
MIDDLES

In a strong second act, both your protagonist and reader feel propelled by forces beyond their control—but what is daunting for the protagonist becomes exhilarating for the reader. In fact there's a direct relationship between the two that's worth highlighting: the more imminent and real the threat to your protagonist in the second act—and the more possible or even probable his failure—the more invested the reader becomes. The plot-level trials your hero faces in the middle of your book reinforce what's personally at stake for him—why he can't simply walk away, why he has to see it through, no turning back. And why the reader has to see it through, too.

But because the second act is the longest and most sustained portion of the book—comprising roughly 50 percent of the total story—there's also the most opportunity for misstep or error, for losing focus or forgetting what's really important to your novel as a whole. A second act that's lost its focus is often described as *sagging*, though a more accurate term might be *floundering*—appearing episodic or fragmented, a collection of events with little apparent connection to or bearing on one another rather than a series of interrelated and unavoidable incidents building in intensity, one upon the next.

A strong second act has the inevitable momentum of a roller coaster, something you white-knuckle your way through and enjoy the ride. Let's consider what constitutes a strong second act and consider some ways to make sure the middle of our story maintains its forward movement and intensity.

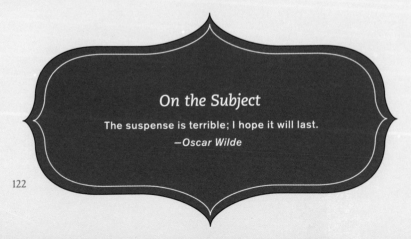

On the Subject

The suspense is terrible; I hope it will last.
—*Oscar Wilde*

CRAFTING &
MAINTAINING SUSPENSE

The success of your second act—if we're to be perfectly honest—really depends upon your ability to toy with the reader. You begin the act with a difficult obstacle for your protagonist to overcome, which he does, offering the character (and reader) a moment of release. Then comes the next obstacle, which is more difficult than the previous and has higher stakes, making it seem more unlikely that the character will, or can, overcome it. And yet, against the odds, he does, and again the reader feels release, the momentary hope that everything's going to be okay. But the reprieve lasts only until the next conflict presents itself, which seems even more difficult to overcome, leading to ever-greater release (perhaps even relief) when the hero does. Which is of course short-lived, because here comes the *next* obstacle, and *this* one …

This is the momentum required of a strong second act, the constant forward motion created by ever-building suspense and release, moving us closer to the book's inevitable conclusion. Let's take a closer look at how suspense shapes and propels Act II.

On the Subject

The suspense of a novel is not only in the reader, but in the novelist, who is intensely curious about what will happen to the hero.
—*Mary McCarthy*

THE SHAPE & FUNCTION OF THE SECOND ACT

In conventional three-act structure, several moments of second-act conflict stand out from the rest: the First Culmination, a moment of conflict that occurs about midway (or sometimes just later) in the act and results in what's called the Darkest Moment, and then Plot Point 2, which again changes the direction of the story and propels us toward the third and final act. As you can see, all three come in the middle-to-end of the act—though their exact placement and proximity to each other depends upon your approach—and serve to focus the conflict, and the reader's sense of anxiety, toward the finale.

The First Culmination is the moment around the midpoint of Act II when it seems like our protagonist is finally within reach of his goal and might actually pull it off, increasing our momentary sense of hope. But as you've likely already guessed—we still have a lot of book left—the protagonist in some way fails to reach the goal, falls short, and the result of all that hope deferred is the Darkest Moment for both the character and reader, the sense that all might really be lost. This is the ultimate toying with the reader's emotions, the ultimate rise and fall all at once.

Nevertheless, the hero isn't beaten yet; he gains new hope and makes one last push toward achieving the goal. This momentary new lease on life, this last turn for the character and the story, is your Plot Point 2. Whether your character *prevails* in this last push, this direct moment of conflict, is the subject of the third act, the Climax of your novel (and the payoff the reader has been waiting for the entire book).

Let's take just a moment to see how our three examples follow second-act structure before we speak more specifically about creating and keeping up suspense in the act.

THE WIZARD OF OZ

First Culmination	Darkest Moment	Plot Point 2
midpoint moment when the protagonist seems within reach of her goal	the result of the protagonist's failure to achieve the goal in the First Culmination; a moment when all seems lost	turning point where the protagonist finds a new direction and/or lease on life, leading to Act III's final conflict and Climax
After meeting up with the Tin Man, Lion, and Scarecrow and encountering numerous obstacles along the way—witch, flying monkeys, poppy fields, etc.—Dorothy finally arrives at the Emerald City to see the Wizard. Looks like Dorothy's about to achieve her goal! Um … right?	The Wizard turns out to be a gigantic grump who refuses to help Dorothy and friends. All that yellow-brick-road-following, flying-monkey dodging, and song singing for nothing.	The Wizard offers a counterproposal: He'll help Dorothy if, and only if, she faces the Wicked Witch of the West and brings the witch's broomstick to him.

THE SILENCE OF THE LAMBS

First Culmination	Darkest Moment	Plot Point 2
midpoint moment when the protagonist seems within reach of her goal	the result of the protagonist's failure to achieve the goal in the First Culmination; a moment when all seems lost	turning point where the protagonist finds a new direction and/or lease on life, leading to Act III's final conflict and Climax
Having found out that the deal Starling made with him for helping on the	Crawford and his SWAT team break down the door to Jame Gumm's	Starling, a bit upset she isn't in Illinois for the catch, decides to follow

Buffalo Bill case was fake, Lecter begins "working" with the director of the hospital for the criminally insane where he's kept, though Starling realizes the information Lecter has given is false. The bulk of the second act details Starling's race against the clock to get information from Lecter that might save Catherine Martin's life.

Starling connects the dots—after some intense mind games with Lecter—and comes up with a suspect, Jame Gumm, who has been making a woman suit ... literally, a suit made of women. But when Starling calls Jack Crawford to share the information, Crawford already has his sights on the suspect. In fact, he's leading a SWAT team to Jame Gumm's house even as they speak.

Looks like they're about to catch the killer and achieve their goal! Um ... right?

Illinois address. They have their man. Except no one is there. The FBI doesn't have him. Though it's possible, Crawford realizes, that Jame Gumm might have the FBI ... Starling, out on her own.

up on a few last boring interviews to make the case against Gumm, who is surely in custody by now, that much more solid. She knocks on the door of one Jack Gordon and is invited inside. Nice enough house, though a little dark. And what's with these moths ...?

This is a chilling turnaround between the Darkest Moment and Plot Point 2, because Starling, the protagonist, has no idea there's even been a Darkest Moment ... though the reader does. Thus, when Starling enters "Jack Gordon's" house, we understand Starling has just taken a turn toward the final confrontation and climax, though it takes Starling a few tense moments to realize it herself.

THE LORD OF THE RINGS: THE FELLOWSHIP OF THE RING

First Culmination	Darkest Moment	Plot Point 2
midpoint moment when the protagonist seems within reach of her goal	the result of the protagonist's failure to achieve the goal in the First Culmination; a moment when all seems lost	turning point where the protagonist finds a new direction and/or lease on life, leading to Act III's final conflict and Climax
Frodo's road trip at the beginning of Act II runs into a great number of potentially deadly conflicts, but it also sees Frodo picking up friends and allies along the way. In Rivendell, Frodo teams up with a number of warriors dedicated to traveling with Frodo and keeping him, and the One Ring, safe on their way to Mordor, a Fellowship of Nine. The Fellowship sets out on their journey and immediately encounters more conflicts, including their difficulty passing the mountain Caradhras due to its treacherous terrain and bad magic. But the group has an alternate plan: go through the mountains via the Mines of Moria, which, while treacherous, will allow them to pass and continue their journey. Looks like Frodo and the Fellowship are closer to	Mines of Moria = bad idea. The Fellowship is overrun by Orcs and a giant, angry cave troll … but neither is as fierce as the Balrog, a brimstone demon the group encounters on the Bridge of Khazad-dûm that seems unstoppable. The Fellowship only manages to escape when the wizard Gandalf faces the demon and sacrifices himself for the rest. Because of his bravery, the group makes it out of the mines alive, barely, but they've been badly beaten, they've lost their friend (devastating for Frodo, and for the reader), and the Fellowship of Nine is down to eight and already coming apart.	Licking their wounds and demoralized, the Fellowship arrives in Lothlórien, home to the Elven queen Galadriel. After resting—and after Frodo has a conversation with Galadriel where she reveals aspects of Frodo's journey to come—the Fellowship leaves Lothlórien for Mordor once again, leading us also to the final act.

achieving their goal! Um ... right? NOTE: Because *LOTR* is a trilogy, we see a slightly different version of the First Culmination here, as Frodo is still two full installments away from his overall goal of reaching Mordor and destroying the Ring.		

Notice that we're summarizing a number of key scenes of conflict, which make up the first part of Act II and play an important role in leading us to the First Culmination, Darkest Moment, and Plot Point 2 of the act.

Think of your own Act II structure in the same way, beginning by identifying those key moments at the *end* of the act, then going back to consider where the act begins for you, as suggested by where Act I leaves off, and brainstorming possibilities for what might bridge the two. Think of a few moments that occur to you and jot the ideas down. Another possibility is to simply start with your first scene of Act II, giving it what it needs as a scene, and then writing the next and the next the same way, seeing how the scene-by-scene approach propels you toward these late-act pivotal moments.

MAINTAINING EFFECTIVE SECOND-ACT SUSPENSE

The second act of a novel is made up of a series of ever-intensifying conflicts and resolutions that keep your reader in alternating, escalating states of anticipation, anxiety, and release. In other words, the second act is about *suspense*, whether psychological, emotional, psychical, or physical, and second-act suspense is most effective when it both builds logically and incrementally and reminds us of what's at stake for the protagonist.

To this first point: You can't simply throw conflicts into the protagonist's way for their own sake and expect that the effect will be meaningful; if you're writing a love story, for example, you obviously can't drop a Martian invasion into the second act just because you think it'll make for some anxious moments. Instead each conflict and resolution suggests or anticipates the next.

So if we're writing that love story—about a boy who falls in love with and tries to woo a girl who belongs to someone else, let's say—then the first major conflict we see in the second act might be the boy trying to impress the girl in some way that backfires: showing up at her job with a dozen roses and a song he's written and interrupting a very important meeting for her. Maybe the next scene is his realizing he'd screwed up and wanting to make it up to her, to show her that he really does care, yet he does so in some grand way that *also* backfires and moves him even further from his goal. He becomes so depressed that he goes to a bar and drinks heavily and ends up talking to a girl who is in no way the love of his life but who, nevertheless, pays him attention and tells him that the other girl ain't worth it, he's too good for her (she says this while smacking gum, I imagine). And so the boy, our hero, drunk and depressed, takes the girl back home with him. No sooner than he gets her inside, his doorbell rings … It's the love of his life, who has been thinking about it and feels bad that she dismissed his earlier, stupid advances (she's secretly become flattered by them; her fiancé is the exact opposite, never paying her any attention). Thus the boy opens the door, there's the love of his life at his doorstep, and suddenly the gum-chewing girl from the bar walks up behind our hero wearing only her t-shirt, calls our hero by the wrong name and then asks, "Who's the broad?"

This is a quick, goofy example, but it still makes the point: The moments of conflict in your second act must build off each other logically, raise the stakes logically, in order to be truly effective. This is why our hero going to a bar and picking up some random girl looks much more dangerous to us, much more suspenseful, than if he'd gone to a bar and fought off ninjas.

This goes along with the second point, that effective suspense must remind us what's personally at stake for your protagonist, must lead back to our character's main motivation or goal (hence why ninjas wouldn't be an effective scene in the previous example—not because ninjas aren't deadly, but because they're not *relevant*, as they have no bearing on our hero's longing for the love of his life). This is why setting up character and motivation is so important in the first act: Everything we see afterward should have a direct relationship to and bearing on that motivation. The most exciting action sequence in the world will ultimately mean nothing if it seems the character has nothing at stake. The ultimate suspense we feel in the second act is, simply, that the protagonist might actually fail in his quest.

Note, too, how the above example contains the elements of second-act structure we just discussed: the First Culmination is the moment when our hero's true love shows up on his doorstep, which is exactly what he's hoped for all along. And this might be the end of the story, a happy ending, except that it's of course doomed: the girl from the bar comes in and snatches defeat from the jaws of victory, and the hero's brokenhearted true love storms off, probably hurling insults and curses back at him such as, "Don't you ever call me again! I'm getting married to George!" Thus, just when it looked like the hero might succeed, now it appears there's no hope whatsoever. Now what's left is that we introduce our Plot Point 2, our hero making one last stand for the love of his life—perhaps interrupting her wedding, à la *The Graduate*, or finishing first in the big race, capturing Bigfoot, discovering Plutonium, whatever he believes will win her back ... We'll have to read to the finale to find out if they'll live happily ever after.

FORGETTING WHERE YOUR STORY STARTED (OR WHERE IT'S HEADED)

The beginning of your novel contains or suggests the ending, and the end reflects and points back to the beginning, but the duty of bridging the two and fulfilling that arc really falls on the *middle*. And as plots naturally become more complicated chapter by chapter, and as events of plot and subplot begin unfolding at a quicker pace and in unexpected new directions in the second act, it can be far too easy to lose sight of what launched the novel in the first place and what related resolution awaits. If you find your novel lacks cohesion in the second act—if the events begin to seem episodic or unrelated, or if it seems that your book has taken on more of a sideways, rather than forward, momentum (hint: if your manuscript is hundreds and hundreds of pages long with dozens of minor characters and you still have a lot of "good stuff" to write before you arrive at that Climax)—you might be suffering from the same problem.

So let's troubleshoot this for a minute. In the first act you established that the thing your protagonist wanted, more than anything else in the world, was to reconcile with his estranged wife, whom he misses and loves dearly. Then, at the end of the first act—at Plot Point 1, perhaps—a mysterious stranger offered your protagonist a million dollars to embark on some dubious quest full of danger and intrigue, which your protagonist gladly and quickly accepted. Ever since then, it's been one misadventure after another, and (whataboutyourwife?) the hero has been dodging bullets, walking away in slow-mo from giant explosions (whataboutyourwife?) and having daring fun, and ... wait, wasn't there something else he wanted? Now what was that again ...?

Motivation problems in the middle of a novel are rarely as egregious as this—thank God—but they are no less problematic when they pop up in your work than in the simple example above. For the most part, muddled motivations come about one of two ways: by a branching plot that gets so far away from where the novel started that the events seem unrelated to the original motivation; or, from a protagonist who comes across opportunities to achieve his motivation or goal in the book and yet doesn't take them, as if the goal never really mattered much to begin with. If you set up that all a protagonist wants is reconciliation with his wife, and then he embarks on a plot that apparently has no relation to that whatsoever, that's a problem. If you set up that all he wants is to reconcile with his wife, and yet, when his wife calls him out of the blue in chapter 3, he says he can't talk right now because *Wheel of Fortune* is on, that's a problem. The events in a novel aren't meaningful to a reader on their own; they're meaningful when the reader views and weighs them in relation to the character's motivation, seeing how they either illuminate or hinder the character's quest. And if the events in your second act seem unrelated to the character's motivation—or, worse, contradictory to it, negating the reader's understanding of character—then what you're left with is just a series of things that happen, not a forward-moving plot.

This isn't to say that every single action in a book should go back to tell us something deep about your protagonist's psyche—the reader isn't going to see him scratch his nose and wonder what that means—but the major events of plot *should* have some relationship to, and some bearing on, the character's motivation and quest, what it is he really wants at heart. The reason for this is simple: Without desire, there can be no conflict. And without conflict, there can be no story.

LEAVING ROOM FOR ORGANIC STORY GROWTH

There's a wonderful quote from the novelist Mary McCarthy on the use of suspense in fiction: suspense for the reader comes first for the *writer*, who is "intensely curious about what will happen next." What this tells us is that the writer, rather than being one who knows everything that will happen, and in what order, has to be open to twists and turns she did not foresee or plan. When the writer knows everything that will happen in a story beforehand, there's no room for her to be surprised—and that lack of surprise and suspense will certainly extend to the reader as well. (In fact, if a writer knows everything that will happen in a story beforehand, I'm not sure why she would bother to write it at all.)

Some of my favorite essays to bring into the creative writing classroom involve this very subject: Flannery O'Connor's "Writing Short Stories," for instance, in which she discusses her story "Good Country People" about a girl with a wooden leg, Hulga, who falls for a con man named Manley Pointer, disguised as a traveling Bible salesman. The story ends with Pointer convincing the

On the Subject

Follow the accident, fear the fixed plan—that is the rule.

—*John Fowles*

girl to detach the leg and show it to him, at which point he puts the leg in his valise before exiting the loft of the barn where he's just stranded poor confused Hulga. When students read the story—the ending of which seems both a shock and absolutely unavoidable—they are typically blown away by O'Connor's admission, in the accompanying essay, that

> I had no idea he was going to steal that wooden leg until ten or twelve lines before he did it, but when I found out that this was what was going to happen, I realized it was inevitable. This is a story that produces a shock for the reader, and I think one reason for this is that it produced a shock for the writer.

The reason they're surprised by O'Connor's admission—beyond the fact that it seems the only way the story could have been ended—is that they believe writers are masterful, genius schemers who plan out every last twist and turn with deliberation. (As a result, these students typically try to plan out their *own* fiction in exacting detail even before they've begun writing, with the result being fiction that contains no surprise or mystery for anyone.) Moreover, they're surprised when a fiction professor, whom they expect will give them the secret to narrative omnipotence and control, tells them they should write by the seat of their pants, not knowing where a story is headed until it actually heads there. You know ... the same way it might seem antithetical to you reading this book.

But the truth of the matter is most writers write by *balancing* conscious control and happy accident. And while a project as daunting as a novel demands you proceed with an overall structure and direction in mind, you should also be welcoming of surprise when it comes along ... so long, of course, as the thing you didn't expect to happen makes the story *better*.

LETTING THE STORY LEAD

For a bit of practice in letting the story lead you, take another look at Worksheet 8: Finding Your Voice on page 241. While the stated goal of the exercise is to help uncover your tendencies and natural strengths in voice, it's also excellent for getting used to writing without overplanning where you're going next, letting a first line inspire and then lead to a second and third and so on.

If it seems like such an exercise would lead to a passage without direction or purpose, try to keep in mind the O'Connor quote on the previous page and trust that your subconscious will help direct the work. In fact, proceeding from a first line and then writing one line at a time might lead you to a few moments of surprise and shock that, in hindsight, you realize you couldn't have planned any better.

RAISING THE STAKES

One of the hurdles you'll face in your story's second act is finding ways to constantly re-raise stakes effectively. If you think of suspense as coming only in big, pulse-pounding moments of action or drama, with each scene being bigger than the last, then you're going to find out that constantly one-upping yourself in this way just isn't sustainable (nor is it truly suspenseful). Pulse-pounding scenes repeating back-to-back cease to be pulse pounding at all; it's like going to see a blockbuster summer movie that has so many car chases, billowing explosions, and hot gunfights that the spectacle becomes boring.

I bring up film because I think the form has had a negative influence on the way many writers think about building suspense and tension in fiction. We're so accustomed to seeing how movies deliver these moments that we lose sight of the fact that *silence* is suspense. (Jonathan Demme, who directed the movie version of *The Silence of the Lambs*, has said the scariest thing a filmmaker can show is a closed door. The terror comes not from seeing what's on the other side but from the anticipation of what *might* be.)

Certainly there's a place for spectacle in fiction, but when you find yourself writing toward those much-anticipated moments of suspense in your second act, consider how turning down the volume could better serve to ratchet up the anxiety and intensity of the scene.

BUILDING SUSPENSE BY LOWERING THE VOLUME

One of the most horrifying moments in Cormac McCarthy's *The Road* comes when the father and son, hungry and desperate, stumble upon an apparently abandoned house, which the father believes—or simply hopes—might have supplies inside. If the father notices anything odd about the house he gives no indication; besides, they're in such straits by this point they can't afford not to go in. The boy, on the other hand, begs for them to keep moving almost as soon as they've spotted the house, in spite of the fact that there's no apparent need to fear. The boy's feeling foreshadows the danger they're about to walk into, an effective tool in building suspense. We're put on edge because the boy is on edge, though neither he nor we know exactly why.

Inside the father and son investigate slowly room by room, deliberately, with McCarthy stretching the tension and time of the scene through stark detail and description: "The ashes were cold. Some blackened pots stood about ... He stood and looked out the window. Gray trampled grass. Gray snow ..." Finally the two come to a pantry where the

On the Subject

The power of stillness: an intensifier, a marker, an ability to define what surrounds it, using antidramatic, antinarrative means.
—*Charles Baxter*

138

father notices a hatch door that's been padlocked; something's valuable enough inside to keep it locked. The father goes out to a dilapidated tool shed and finds a spade he can use to pry off the lock while the boy continues begging for them to leave.

Once the father breaks the lock, he and the boy open the hatch and descend inside:

> He started down the rough wooden steps. He ducked his head and then flicked the lighter and swung the flame out over the darkness like an offering. Coldness and damp. An ungodly stench. The boy clutched at his coat. He could see part of a stone wall. Clay floor. An old mattress darkly stained. He crouched and stepped down again and held out the light. Huddled against the back wall were naked people, male and female, all trying to hide, shielding their faces with their hands. On the mattress lay a man with his legs gone to the hip and the stumps of them blackened and burnt. The smell was hideous.
>
> Jesus, he whispered.
>
> Then one by one they turned and blinked in the pitiful light. Help us, they whispered. Please help us.
>
> Christ, he said. Oh Christ.
>
> He turned and grabbed the boy. Hurry, he said. Hurry.
>
> He dropped the lighter. No time to look. He pushed the boy up the stairs. Help us, they called.
>
> Hurry.
>
> A bearded face appeared blinking at the foot of the stairs. Please, he called. Please.
>
> Hurry. For God's sake hurry.
>
> He shoved the boy through the hatch and sent him sprawling. He stood and got hold of the door and swung it

over and let it slam down and he turned to grab the boy but
the boy had gotten up and was doing his little dance of terror.
For the love of God will you come on, he hissed. But the boy
was pointing out the window and when he looked he went
cold all over. Coming across the field toward the house were
four bearded men and two women. He grabbed the boy by
the hand. Christ, he said. Run. Run.

Our too-automatic tendency in writing such a scene would be to make
it loud, clumsy, and chaotic, like a scene from a hostage movie or a
bank heist (Now-now-now!-Move-move-move!-Let's-go!-Let's-go!). Mc-
Carthy goes the opposite direction, and it's the chilling quiet of the
scene that makes it all the more terrifying and claustrophobic, aided
by the deliberate pacing, the dark images, and the strange understatement of such an intense, stomach-dropping moment. The same can
be said for the scenes on either side of it, too—before, the father and
son searching the house, and after, the two hiding in the tall weeds
barely outside the house, the father trying to suppress a cough that
would give them away, as the four bearded men and two women come
looking for them. Turning down the volume turns up the tension.

RAISING TENSION THROUGH DIALOGUE

Tension-raising dialogue works the same way; it's too easy, and also wrongheaded, to think that important moments of conflict have to be shouting matches, the same way hysterical characters spit their lines toward each other in bad TV melodramas. Again, it's restraint and silence in dialogue—the not-said—that often reveals the true depth of tension in a conversation, even more so than what's actually said.

The classic example is Ernest Hemingway's short story "Hills Like White Elephants," which is delivered almost entirely in (understated) dialogue. The two characters in the story are an American couple traveling abroad in order to procure a medical procedure that neither will directly state—but which the reader discerns—is an abortion. The levels of the not-said in the characters' conversation also reveal the strained state of the relationship and the imbalance of power. Though, again, these are things the characters never directly state, likely because they don't want to admit it to themselves:

On the Subject

Arguments are most nerve-wracking when the characters imply what they feel instead of coming right out and saying it ... If you're trying to build pressure, don't take the lid off the pot.

—*Jerome Stern*

"It's really an awfully simple operation, Jig," the man said. "It's not really an operation at all."

The girl looked at the ground the table legs rested on.

"I know you wouldn't mind it, Jig. It's really not anything. It's just to let the air in."

The girl did not say anything.

"'I'll go with you and I'll stay with you all the time. They just let the air in and then it's all perfectly natural."

"Then what will we do afterwards?"

"We'll be fine afterwards. Just like we were before."

"What makes you think so?"

"That's the only thing that bothers us. It's the only thing that's made us unhappy."

The girl looked at the bead curtain, put her hand out and took hold of two of the strings of beads.

"And you think then we'll be all right and be happy."

"I know we will. You don't have to be afraid. I've known lots of people that have done it."

"So have I," said the girl. "And afterwards they were all so happy."

"Well," the man said, "if you don't want to you don't have to. I wouldn't have you do it if you didn't want to. But I know it's perfectly simple."

"And you really want to?"

"I think it's the best thing to do. But I don't want you to do it if you don't really want to."

"And if I do it you'll be happy and things will be like they were and you'll love me?"

"I love you now. You know I love you."

"I know. But if I do it, then it will be nice again if I say things are like white elephants, and you'll like it?"

"I'll love it. I love it now but I just can't think about it … ."

What's not being said in this scene are the very things the two *should* be saying—the deeper problems in their relationship, their dueling thoughts on the operation, the subtle coercion on the man's part in convincing Jig to go through with it—and yet we, as readers, understand what's not being said perfectly; the not-said is what makes the scene tense and ultimately heartbreaking. Notice, too, just how much emotion is evident, but restrained, in the scene. Hemingway gets at this very simply: There are no big outbursts, no wild accusations ... No one even raises a voice. Furthermore the dialogue tags aren't loaded with fake bristling emotion via adverbs—she said tearfully, he said bitingly, etc. In fact the tags only seem to be used, when they're used, to make sure we don't lose track of who is speaking. The understatement and quietness of the scene are what create the anxiety. We almost *wish* they'd raise their voices to break the tension—which is, of course, why Hemingway refuses to.

Look for opportunities in your second act to create tension in the same way: by getting quiet and using silence to build suspense.

INEFFECTIVE DIALOGUE

Dialogue, for whatever reason, seems to give many young writers fits. Maybe this stems from the fact that such writers believe that their novels have several voices: the one that emerges from narration and then many different ones that belong to the characters. And to a certain degree this is correct: Your characters should have recognizable voices that emerge in conversation to reveal who they are. But these voices shouldn't really be separate from—incongruous with—the voice in narration.

In fact, it might be helpful to think of dialogue as an extension of narration rather than an interruption of it. Dialogue isn't "real" in that it approximates the way we speak in real life, which, if we were to transcribe it accurately, would be far too redundant and uninspired for the page. Instead, dialogue is stylized speech—polished, precise, and rhythmic. And when it is well styled, well crafted, the dialogue becomes authentic to us, in part because of its distinctiveness. It's so specific and stylized and concrete, the reader accepts it as real.

Technically speaking, all dialogue is filtered through narration; it's not as if a narrator gives us only the paragraphs and then disappears whenever a character opens his mouth (the fact that dialogue has quotation marks around it even signals it's being quoted rather than directly spoken). It's styled the same way that images and metaphors are styled through narration: with specific goals in mind, to create the illusion of a reality, to create verisimilitude. How you craft a particular bit of dialogue depends upon knowing who your characters are and what they want, but it also has to do with what meaning you intend to convey from the conversation and how best to show it.

Consider the following example from Grace Paley's short story "A Conversation with My Father" in which the narrator, a writer, attempts to construct a "happy" story for her dying father, which isn't entirely successful:

First my father was silent, then he said, "Number One: You have a nice sense of humor. Number Two: I see you can't tell a plain story. So don't waste time." Then he said sadly, "Number Three: I suppose that means she was alone, she was left like that, his mother. Alone. Probably sick?"

I said, "Yes."

"Poor woman. Poor girl, to be born in a time of fools, to live among fools. The end. The end. You were right to put that down. The end."

I didn't want to argue, but I had to say, "Well, it is not necessarily the end, Pa."

"Yes," he said, "what a tragedy. The end of a person."

"No, Pa," I begged him. "It doesn't have to be. She's only about forty. She could be a hundred different things in this world as time goes on. A teacher or a social worker. An ex-junkie! Sometimes it's better than having a master's in education."

"Jokes," he said. "As a writer that's your main trouble. You don't want to recognize it. Tragedy! Plain tragedy! Historical tragedy! No hope. The end."

"Oh, Pa," I said. "She could change."

"In your own life, too, you have to look it in the face." He took a couple of nitroglycerin. "Turn to five," he said, pointing to the dial on the oxygen tank. He inserted the tubes into his nostrils and breathed deep. He closed his eyes and said, "No."

The occasion for the conversation, the motivation of the characters, is simple—tell me a "true" story—but the interaction of the two characters through dialogue creates a full emotional weight in the scene. Notice how stylized the dialogue really is, particularly the father's lines: the repetition as he considers the story ("The end. The end. You were right to put that down."), his occasional exhortations or declarations ("Poor girl, to be born in a time of fools, to live among fools."), even the stark effect of his simple last line, uttered seemingly apropos of nothing as he inserts his oxygen tubes and breathes: "No." The dialogue is at once particular to the individual characters—the narrator making uncomfortable jokes to try to lighten the situation, the father calling her out—yet similar in terms of delivery, cadence, and mood. In fact the dialogue sounds like it could be part of the narration; we could remove the quotation marks and streamline it into paragraphs without losing the effect.

Again, practically speaking, these are lines you're unlikely to hear spoken in real life. Think back to the last time you visited someone in a hospital; had there been a man there in his powder-blue gown sitting up in bed and exclaiming, "What a tragedy, the end of a person!" you would've probably backed away, thinking the poor man nuts. But in the context of a story, this stylized dialogue seems real to us. We don't put it up against a picture of what a real man in the hospital would look like, but we certainly picture—and hear—what this man is like. The dialogue creates a convincing illusion of reality. (And it also, in spots, breaks your heart.)

Think of your own dialogue in the same way: not as outside, interrupting voices entering the text but as extensions of your narrative voice. You might even get the hang of crafting dialogue by omitting the quotation marks and thinking of the character's voices as being filtered or channeled through your primary narrative voice. Hopefully what emerges will be as focused and precise as all other aspects of your narration, while also being distinctive to your individual characters and their personalities.

For more practice in crafting dialogue, turn to Worksheet 18 on page 252.

PACING: HOW TO KEEP YOUR PLOT (AND READER) MOVING FORWARD

For whatever reason—maybe because our natural impulse as human beings is to avoid conflict, when our tendency as a novelist should be to welcome it and rush toward it—too many inexperienced writers linger on those moments that are of no real consequence in a story while rushing over or summarizing those moments that should be built up. In such cases, we'll see pages of driving to a destination, with a protagonist thinking about what might happen there, or thinking about what just happened, and we'll also stop at traffic lights, go through a drive-thru, listen to the car stereo. Then, when the protagonist finally arrives, instead of embracing the conflict in the scene and letting us stay in the moment, the writer will rush over, gloss over, or summarize the information the scene is designed to give us so that he can get the hero quickly back in the car and out of there ... having the character think some more about what just happened as he looks for another drive-thru.

On the Subject

I try to leave out the parts that people skip.

—*Elmore Leonard*

A lot happens in your character's day that's of absolutely no importance to us as readers. Think of Jack Bauer in the TV show 24 (but only for a moment, please). Does this man never stop at a bathroom? No time for a sandwich? I think we can assume he does eventually stop his running around, gun-pointing, and cell-phone-yelling to take care of the mundane necessities, but the directors and writers wisely choose to show Bauer in moments of conflict and drama, with brief moments of repose and release to catch our breaths and to suggest the next conflict he'll face. A full episode devoted to his looking for a nearby Starbucks when there's never one around is about as compelling as when I spend a half-hour looking for one. Far less so, in fact, because my coffee fix is not on the line.

This is not to say that every scene in your novel must contain a lit fuse snaking toward explosion, or at least not literally. Quiet, mundane moments are important, too, as we've already seen—as long as they show us something of the character, situation, or what's at stake. But when you catch your character ambling, just doing things because he can, as if bored, then it's time to tighten the tension by either refocusing the scene or doing away with it altogether.

Here are a few tools you might use to keep your pacing tight and your reader's attention focused:

The powers of time and space. When you or I have to get across town, in real life, then we have to grab our keys and wallet, get to the car and crank it up, find a good radio station, obey traffic laws, spend twenty minutes navigating the freeway and getting honked at, finally arrive, find a parking space, pat our pocket for our cell phone, get out of the car, go back to the car because we forgot to lock it, etc. In other words, in real life we are bound by the laws of matter, time, and space.

But as a writer, you are not bound by them. You don't need to show your character drive across town if you don't want to. You don't even need to show him walk across a room unless it suits your needs. That's because in fiction, you control time and space ... and you do so with a few indispensable tools:

- *White space.* We tend to think of dark space, the print, as the really important part of a narrative, but the way you use white space is every bit as important. First, it's aesthetically pleasing, offering the eyes a moment of much-needed rest. It offers the reader a moment of rest, too, a space to take a breath before moving on to the next scene. It's also the ultimate end punctuation mark, forcing us to slow down and remain on a particular point, moment, or line and really take it in. There can be nothing more uplifting, nor more devastating (in a good way), than a sharp, powerful, well-delivered line followed by a bit of pure white page.

  And, in the context of time, space, and pacing, white space is your very own *Star Trek* transporter. Need a character to go a dry cleaner clear across town? White space, then first line of the next scene: *He walked in, rang the bell for service, and then took a number, even though he was the only person there.*

  Needless to say, white space can be your best friend in minimizing what's not important—even getting rid of it altogether—and maximizing what is.

- *Chapter breaks.* The end of a chapter should feel like a completion, a satisfying conclusion to that particular problem or arc, but it should also urge the reader on, should contain enough mystery and promise and excitement to make her, even though it's late, think, "Well, maybe just one more ..."

  That doesn't mean that you should end every chapter with a kind of cliffhanger, like a Saturday-morning serial from the 40s. What it means is that the answer you provide at the end of a chapter raises another question that propels your narrative, tempts the reader to keep going, and keeps up the momentum—the pacing—of your work.

- *Transitions.* Sometimes a single word is enough to keep your fiction active and forward-moving, as is the case with the relatively simple transitions *before, after, later, eventually, subsequently,* and more like them. Transitions like these are shortcuts to future events or quick trips back to past ones, bypassing the tedious or unimportant moments between but still giving a proper sense of time and perspective. If you're in the present moment and know you need something to happen later on with your character, see how easy it is to begin your next line "Later, he ..." or "Later on, when he ..." I know this seems too easy, but you'll be surprised just how much material you'll be able to cover this way, and cover simply.

The power of the subjective focus. Manipulating the powers of time and space is one excellent way to control the pacing of your novel, but you also control the focus of your work: what to zoom in on, what to pull back from, what to minimize and maximize.

- *The iceberg.* Writers don't build a reality by showing everything going on but by being selective with what they show, choosing a few specific images or details that have the effect of standing in for and creating the illusion of the whole. The metaphor used to describe this principle is the iceberg; all we really see of an iceberg is the tip, a small part of it, but from that small part, we understand the enormity of what lies beneath.

    To illustrate, think about how you'd describe a place you enjoy going to, or that you dislike. If you were to describe either one to a friend—let's call the place a coffee shop—you wouldn't begin by saying, "Well, there's a door, and you go in that door, and then there's a floor and you walk on that. Right by the door on the right there's a station with half and half and 2% and sugar and fake sugar and napkins and wooden stirrers, and on the other side of the door is a metal trash can with a black bag sticking out the top, and just inside the door on the one side are two tables with four wooden chairs each and two windows, and on the other side of the aisle are three plush chairs ... ." Instead, you'd choose the specific details that help make your bigger point about the place and how you hate it, let's say—the yellow lighting, the lack of seating, the yuppie businessman booming into his cell phone like he's talking to someone in outer space—and you'd let those few specifics create the whole experience.

- *Showing and telling.* "Show, don't tell," like "write what you know," is misleading advice, and writers who take the advice literally, who think they should show everything and tell nothing, are really doing themselves a disservice.

  Every writer shows and tells, both—it's the proper balance of these that creates meaning. A good example comes from John Cheever's short story "The Enormous Radio," which from the beginning balances both showing and telling to give us a picture of the protagonists, Jim and Irene Westcott:

  > Jim and Irene Westcott were the kind of people who seem to strike that satisfactory average of income, endeavor, and respectability that is reached by the statistical reports in college alumni bulletins. They were the parents of two young children, they had been married nine years, they lived on the twelfth floor of an apartment house near Sutton Place, they went to the theatre on an average

of 10.3 times a year, and they hoped someday to live in Westchester. Irene Westcott was a pleasant, rather plain girl with soft brown hair and a wide, fine forehead upon which nothing at all had been written, and in the cold weather she wore a coat of fitch skins dyed to resemble mink. You could not say that Jim Westcott looked younger than he was, but you could at least say of him that he seemed to feel younger. He wore his graying hair cut very short, he dressed in the kind of clothes his class had worn at Andover, and his manner was earnest, vehement, and intentionally naïve.

The Westcotts are people who want to be part of a certain social class—or who at least want to be perceived that way—and Cheever uses some fine showing to help make the point (the best example: that Irene dyes her fitchskin coat so it looks like mink). But notice just how much of this paragraph involves telling: that they strive for the kind of respectable average one finds in "college alumni bulletins," showing their awareness of status and meeting it; that Irene has a wide forehead "on which nothing at all had been written"; that Jim struck a manner that was "intentionally naïve." All of these give the reader a greater sense of who the Westcotts are, what they value, while at the same time offering sly commentary on them, revealing aspects of their personality and attitudes that the Westcotts wouldn't, and probably couldn't, tell us about themselves. And it accomplishes this much more quickly and efficiently, by combining showing and telling, than showing alone could.

- *Balancing narration and dialogue.* Long stretches of either narration or dialogue have the same effect on a reader: boredom, leading the reader to start scanning, looking for keywords to get through the passage rather than really reading. Look out for long passages of straight narration or uninterrupted dialogue in your work, and when you find them, look for ways to balance the two to keep the pace quick and forward-moving and to get across information through interaction rather than summary or soliloquy.

SKETCHING ACT II

Turn to Worksheet 19: Act II Bridging Scenes on page 253 and briefly sketch out your ideas for scenes that might begin the second act, leading ever closer to the act's Final Culmination and Darkest Moment. Don't feel constrained by putting these scenes down on paper; rather, simply remind yourself where Act I ended, consider what moments of conflict and resolution present themselves, and then brainstorm how and when you might hit those moments in Act II.

When you've finished the sketch, take a look at Worksheet 20: Raising the Stakes on page 254 and run one of your scene ideas through the questions you find there, considering how to keep the tension in the scene high and the pacing tight. When you have a good idea of the arc and desired feel of the scene, write it—limiting yourself to 2,000 focused words—trying to incorporate the ideas in this section: building the suspense and intensity of the scene by lowering the volume; balancing showing and telling, narration and dialogue; and keeping the proverbial lid on the pot.

COMPLICATING YOUR CHARACTERS

You might be afraid that simple motivations lead to simplistic characters—that once you've discovered what your character really wants is, say, a big piece of cheesecake, all he or she has to do is run through your novel screaming, "I want cheesecake!" (Detective 1: "This is a grisly crime scene, Fred. One of the worst. I'm afraid we've got a serial killer on our hands here." Detective 2: "But what about *cheesecake?!?*")

That's not the case, of course. Complex characters can, do, and should emerge from the simplest of motivations, and there are two main reasons for this:

1. Even guided by simple motivations, our actions in pursuit of those motivations are complex, even occasionally contradictory or self-defeating.
2. Simple motivations don't mean necessarily *pure or noble*.

The prime example of both of these is Melville's Captain Ahab, who has one, and only one, single-minded motivation: to kill the white

On the Subject

Fiction is the art form of human yearning ... the elements of the plot come from thwarted or blocked or challenged attempts to fulfill that yearning.
—*Robert Olen Butler*

whale that stole his leg. But his actions in trying to achieve this goal are terrifying, risking not just his own life and his ship but the lives of his entire crew, just to appease his own need for vengeance. And while his motivation is clear, it is anything but noble, fueled by some of the worst—and most prevalent—instincts in man. His straightforward motivation leads to actions that reveal the complexity, the darker side, of human nature.

But even with a character like Frodo in *The Lord of the Rings*, who has a rather pure motivation, the conflicts he faces and the actions he takes reveal his complexity. Frodo is not an epic hero, greater than us. He is fragile, vulnerable, and occasionally makes the wrong move, in spite of the fact that he's doing his best, and for the right reason; he's even occasionally tempted by the One Ring to keep it for himself and use its power. To put it another way, he's like us. And this is why Tolkien gives Frodo the Ring rather than, say, the warrior-king Aragorn. Aragorn comes very close to being larger than life in the trilogy, and in his strong hands we might feel that taking the One Ring to Mordor is a done deal. Instead Tolkien hands the One Ring to a hobbit—small in size, big in heart, no expert in combat, seemingly the character in the novel *least* likely to hold it. This is the reason we connect with the story. There is something at risk in handing the Ring to Frodo ... and because there's real risk, there's also real reason to *hope* for a good outcome.

Let's consider how to complicate your own characters in the same way: by imbuing them with desire and then putting obstacles in their way (including, of course *themselves*).

CHARACTER DEEPENING (PART I): THE PROTAGONIST

At the beginning of the book, your main character is defined by his internal motivation: what your character values and wants. But as you begin moving him through the events in the novel—facing conflicts, facing other characters—you'll start to see him as a full human being, someone who wants something but does not always act in ways that will achieve the goal, or that will be in his best interests.

Let's return to the hypothetical example (from page 129) of a man who tries to woo the love of his life away from another, a pretty clear and straightforward motivation. But if you recall, we had our hypothetical character messing up in almost every way: he shows up to his would-be lover's work to serenade her and interrupts an important meeting; maybe he hires a skywriter to announce his love from on high, via smoke message, but the pilot is drunk and misspells her name, or writes something obscene; finally we put him in a bar where he is wooed by another girl, takes her back home, and then has his true love show up at his doorstep to witness

On the Subject

My characters really dictate themselves to me. I am not free of them, really, and I can't force them into situations they themselves haven't willed ... yet, at the onset, at least, I determine the characters.

—*Joyce Carol Oates*

the transgression, seemingly strike three. Though the same simple motivation is present throughout, our poor character—like all our poor characters—is only human, meaning he makes mistakes, underreacts or overreacts, misjudges in epic fashion. He tries his best, fails, tries again, and in the process he becomes real.

This is the same approach all writers take in building our characters: Start from the baseline and then test the character, seeing how she acts and reacts. And when you've set up character clearly at the start and then partway into the book find her beginning to say or do things that surprise you, don't fret but rejoice. The character has begun to reveal herself to you as a full person, catching you off guard in terms of who she is and what she's capable of. This is perfectly acceptable and, in fact, cause for celebration ... as long as her ultimate goal or motivation remains the thing driving her actions.

DEEPENING THROUGH BACKSTORY

Backstory is an important part of developing complex characters, offering a sense of depth, a sense that our characters are real people with lives and pasts of their own (that often have a bearing on the present problems faced in the novel). But backstory can also be tricky for a writer: It's far too easy to flash back to the past and then find yourself stuck there, wondering how in the world you're going to get back to the future, or to feel the need to identify and explain *every* past action that's had a bearing on the current situation. Part of this comes from our psychology-influenced culture, which tends to see our actions and personalities as the result of past events and traumas, and certainly the contemporary fiction writer has come under the same influence, has been trained to find the difficult childhood experience, for example, that now explains why your character is a philanderer, addict, martyr, murderer, or saint. It's part of our times.

But even more than a reflection of the contemporary mind-set, effective backstory is valuable in that it furthers our story's sense of *verisimilitude*, that our characters, and even our larger fictional world, really exist. A person without

On the Subject

About a flashback scene ... ask first if it is absolutely necessary. Be firm about this. The information we get in the flashback must come that way because that's the best way to present it.
—*James Scott Bell*

a past is perhaps common to slasher films and spaghetti westerns, but in the real world the places we go and people we meet all have a discernable (or at least assumed) history, depth, and perspective. Adding these dimensions to our characters and fictional world makes both seem more real to a reader. However, when our narrative seems to be *stuck* in the past or obsessed with it, the sense of verisimilitude is destroyed, and the reader is left wondering which "story" is really the important one: the one in the past, or the one in the present.

The first step in balancing backstory is recognizing that it really falls into two different categories: incidental and direct.

Incidental backstory is used primarily for purposes of description, to deepen our immediate understanding of a person, place, or thing. I call this kind "incidental" to make the point that, while this is often quite useful in establishing verisimilitude in your fiction, you've *chosen* to give backstory as a way of making the person, place, or thing relatable, even though you might've done the same work by using a different tack.

A good example of incidental backstory comes early in Jeffrey Eugenides' *The Virgin Suicides* in which the first-person plural narrators—a group of neighborhood boys who are now men in their thirties—recall the fateful summer from their youths when the Lisbon girls, five beautiful sisters from their community, took their own lives. Because the boys were outside the Lisbon home and thus never had the intimate access to know what, exactly, was going on behind closed doors, the narrators have had to piece the account together from second-hand sources like their friend Paul Baldino, the son of a reputed mobster, who claimed to have been inside the Lisbon home the night of the first Lisbon girl's suicide attempt. To explain *how* Baldino was inside the home, Eugenides gives this brief bit of incidental backstory:

> A few years earlier, behind the spiked Baldino fence patrolled by two identical white German shepherds, a group of workmen had appeared one morning. They hung tarpaulins over ladders to

obscure what they did, and after three days, when they whisked the tarps away, there, in the middle of the lawn, stood an artificial tree trunk. It was made of cement, painted to look like bark, complete with fake knothole and two lopped limbs pointing at the sky with the fervor of amputee stubs. In the middle of the tree, a chainsawed wedge contained a metal grill.

Paul Baldino said it was a barbecue, and we believed him. But, as time passed, we noticed that no one ever used it … Soon the rumor began to circulate that the tree trunk was an escape tunnel, that it led to a hideaway along the river where Sammy the Shark kept a speedboat … Then, a few months after the rumors began, Paul Baldino began emerging in people's basements, through the storm sewers.

The backstory here, as you can see, serves a specific descriptive, atmospheric, and logistical purpose, and it does the trick wonderfully, but is it strictly *necessary* to give this bit of history? No. All Eugenides needs to do is to find some way to put Paul Baldino inside the Lisbon home in order for him to report on his finding Cecelia, the oldest Lisbon girl, in the bathtub with her wrists cut. Eugenides could manage the same without giving this story of mobsters and secret passageways; he could just as easily have Baldino be a Peeping Tom, or a cat burglar, or have him parachute in from the sky. The incidental backstory is a choice—an artful one that provides the reader with another glimpse of the town and its inhabitants, another piece of local folklore to add depth to the collective voice. The reason we, as authors, *choose* to go with incidental backstory is because we think it does the trick *best*, though we recognize we might accomplish the same thing without involving history at all.

Direct backstory, on the other hand, has a crucial bearing on, and relevance to, the present action in the story—information that's substantive rather than descriptive or atmospheric. The burden of this kind of backstory, since it's needed for the reader's full understanding of the character, is to find interesting ways of delivering it so that it doesn't feel like an information dump or summary. In fact, all past action that you bring into your story has to be delivered with as much focus and momentum as the present action; even when we're in the past, the reader has to be invested in the present narrative moment.

Of course there are many ways of delivering direct backstory. Sometimes you'll want to flash back and give us the past event in scene. Other times direct backstory might be revealed through quick asides in the narration, or in dialogue between characters, or in subtle actions or reactions of the character to certain situations that suggest the deeper thing beneath. It's really up to you in terms of how you give the past what it requires, but make sure whatever time you spend going backwards in time is for the right reason: to move your story *forward*.

The biggest hurdle most writers have in balancing backstory is confusing incidental backstory and direct backstory, spending pages in the past building up some moment they *believe* to be important but that's really more descriptive or atmospheric. My favorite example of what seems to be direct backstory, but is revealed to be incidental, comes from Vladimir Nabokov's *Lolita*, wherein the predatory Humbert Humbert wants to dissuade the reader from dwelling too much on, and psychoanalyzing, the untimely death of his young mother:

> My very photogenic mother died in a freak accident (picnic, lightning) when I was three …

No need to whip the wind around, blow the checkered tablecloth into the air, or cull dark clouds into thunderheads when "(picnic, lightning)" does the trick. Sometimes, of course, your backstory will be more substantive and will require pages, precision, and patience. But sometimes it will be incidental, requiring only "(picnic, lightning)." As you think about your own ideas regarding backstory, make sure you can differentiate between these and know when each is really called for.

CHARACTER DEEPENING (PART II): CRAFTING AN ANTAGONIST

In certain situations and genres, the conflict your protagonist faces might take the form of a person—an antagonist—standing in the main character's way. Antagonists walk a peculiar line: In one sense they clearly fall into the category of supporting character, as their existence helps define our protagonist and his quest more clearly; yet antagonists also feel like major characters and sometimes even threaten to steal the show. This is especially the case with books or stories in a series, where the hero stays the same and the villain changes with each new installment; the tendency can be to do something dynamic with each new antagonist to add variety, and as a result the villains become increasingly more outrageous and scene-stealing even as the protagonist holds steady and perhaps begins to look a little washed-out by comparison.

There are two things to remember—and keep in stride—when crafting an antagonist. The first is that the

On the Subject

Villains make the hero, and the reader, squirm in anguish.
—*Jessica Page Morrell*

antagonist is, like every other major and minor character in your book, a full person with his own motivations, wants, and goals. Your antagonist can't be an unchecked want, one-dimensional. Even if his goal is straightforward and simple, it just so happens that his earnest want or goal is in direct conflict with what your protagonist wants (and thus what *we* want to happen in the story). The villain, as you'll sometimes hear said, is the hero of his own story. He's going after a goal just as your hero is, no matter how misguided his motivation.

Now for the second thing to remember: The villain may be the hero of his own story, but this story ain't it. Because we see everything in your fictional world through the lens and perspective of your protagonist, the antagonist is clearly in opposition, clearly a hurdle. If we wanted to—and now we're playing the role of critic, or maybe therapist, for just a minute—we could see the antagonist's side of things. But for the most part we're *not* inclined, because we want the protagonist, the hero, to succeed.

Those of you working in genres may be hesitant to think of your antagonist as a person—if you're writing a mystery where there's a sadistic killer on the loose, for example, you don't want to condone sadism by making your killer an otherwise okay guy. Or if you're working in epic fantasy or science fiction or horror, you want your bad guys to be bad guys, darn it, as close to pure evil as you can manage. To this point I'll say, the needs of your story and genre certainly *will* affect the way you craft an antagonist, but I'd beware of making your villain the embodiment of pure evil for the same reason you should avoid making your protagonist an exemplar of pure virtue: The reader can't identify with such extremes since none of us are pure evil or pure good. Thus, at a baseline, your antagonist must be in some way *attractive* to the reader, in some subversive way seductive, so that rather than being repelled by him we're intrigued enough to move closer, even if we're thankful we can shut the book if we ever get *too* close. Besides, unchecked evil isn't very frightening; the reader can simply say, *Well, I'm not ever going to encounter that.* But evil that shows up with a smile, and then knocks you over the head, is terrifying. That's the kind of evil we *might* encounter ... and that's a thought that could keep us up at night.

The most important thing to keep in mind is that this is the protagonist's story. And even if your antagonist is a fuller character than the *other* secondary characters in the book, or gets more page time, he's still there to help us see, understand, and ultimately sympathize with the hero even better.

OVERACTIVE OR INACTIVE SUPPORTING CHARACTERS

If in the second act you find your novel veering off course either because a minor character has come in and tried to run the place, or because your minor characters seem to be doing nothing but sitting on your couch, eating your food, not really contributing, you should put them to the test: determine why they're there, if they can be brought in line somehow, or, if not, how you might excise them from the novel.

Minor characters who become personal "darlings" for the author can be *very* hard to kill, and often a writer will find some way to justify keeping around an inactive but favorite minor character based on very thin reasoning, such as saying that the character adds comic relief (yes, but comic relief to your depressing post-apocalyptic gothic revenge story?) or that the character adds a romantic element (yes, but does your chainsaw-murderer bipolar anti-hero really *need* a love interest?) or, or … .

If an inactive supporting character does indeed seem to fulfill some function like this—but is otherwise inert—you might see if another and better-established supporting character could fulfill that role just as easily. Or you might consider streamlining several supporting characters into just one who does the trick.

Ultimately who stays and goes is not up to you as the author but up to your story. When in doubt, try to listen to what the story is telling you to do and follow that advice; it's almost always going to be right. As for *over*active secondary characters—those who seem intent on making their story the novel's big one—see the section Overactive or Inactive Subplots on page 175 for tips on getting them under control.

165

UPPING THE READER'S EMOTIONAL INVESTMENT

The reason we begin our novel in the internal motivation of the protagonist—and the reason we're continually reminded of that motivation as we move through the external conflicts faced by the protagonist—is because this is how our reader directly and emotionally relates to the quest. Few, if any, of our readers will have ever faced the specific external conflicts we make our character face in the novel, but all of them will have faced the *internal* motivation and conflicts associated with the character's external quest: Wanting to protect someone we love, and not knowing if we can. Wanting to win someone's heart, and not knowing if we will. Wanting to be happy, safe, accepted, appreciated, loved, more. These are things *all* of us want at our core, and when these are put in jeopardy by the conflicts your character faces, the reader feels the anxiety, too.

Taken to their conclusion at the end of the novel, these familiar wants and needs, put at risk through conflict and confrontation, begin to form the bigger organizing principle of theme, which we'll discuss at greater length in

On the Subject

Push your characters to the edge, and you will pull your readers close.
—*Donald Maass*

Part Three. But as you navigate the long second act of your book, trying to keep up forward momentum and raise the stakes, it's important that you continue to make the connection back to the character as a person, back to what he wants and what's really at risk. Think back to those books that most affected *you* as a reader: What was it about the character's struggle that you felt *personally* connected to, that moved you to either anger or tears? What were the specific moments in those books where you felt most exhilarated and full of hope or where you feared that all was lost? Do you still think about those moments? Can you still conjure the emotion you felt as you read?

When the events in your book matter in some meaningful way to your protagonist, they become meaningful to the reader, and the reader will bring her own personal experiences, hopes, and fears to bear on the text. Furthermore the reader *wants* to—the intimate, personal relationship engendered by narrative is unlike an audience's relationship to any other art form. It feels intimate and real.

Let it.

TAKING STOCK OF CHARACTERS

try it out

If you're wondering why some of these questions of character-deepening are coming this late, into the second act, let me assure you there's a clear reason for this: loading your protagonist with too much baggage at the beginning of a novel tends only to weigh him, and your story, down and can make for a sluggish start to a book. But beginning with a clear and simple goal, and then watching how the character faces conflicts in pursuit of that goal, offers the reader the chance to really discover who the character is and the author the chance to build and reveal the character's complexity as a human being scene by scene.

Now is the proper time to take stock of the character—how we see him changing, for better or worse, what we understand about him more clearly now than perhaps we did early on, what's really on the line for him as we move toward the pivotal moments at the end of the act that will propel him toward the finale. To that end, take a look at Worksheet 21: Deepening the Protagonist on page 255 and answer the questions you find there. Every challenge the protagonist has faced to this point has revealed a little more of who he is and what he's made of. And the biggest challenges are just ahead.

PIVOTAL SCENES: PLOTTING AND PACING

There are a number of reasons why your midpoint scenes might be a little less captivating than those at the beginning of your novel: You might be fatigued by this point and not as focused on the word-by-word as with the finish line (which happens to all of us). Or, you might find yourself rushing through certain scenes—those revealing direct backstory, for instance, or developing character relationships—in order to get to the "bigger" moments of action and plot we discussed at the beginning of Part Two.

But the fact is, while there are indeed major and minor scenes in a novel, there are no *small* scenes; each new scene is an opportunity to reinvest your reader in the world of your story. Scene breaks are a breather, a quick chance for the reader to rest up, but the very next scene should pull the reader in again and entice her to stay with the same energy and focus as the previous scene ... or the novel's *first* scene, for that matter. Thinking about the big picture is important, and perhaps inevitable the closer you get to that third and final act, but don't focus on the big picture to the exclusion of the scene right in front of you—or, more to the point, the one right in front of the reader. Whatever the reader's looking at right now, in any given moment and on any given page, is the most important writing you've done.

That's not to say that every word you put down in a first draft has to be, or even could be, perfect; it can't, and you'll certainly have time (a lot of it) to polish up the work in revision later on. Nevertheless, when individual scenes start lagging, so does the book as a whole, and you don't want to start veering off course in the second act by rushing through scenes that deserve your focus and attention, whether major or minor.

KEEPING YOUR SCENES KINETIC

Let's take just a moment to remind ourselves of some fundamentals of scene-making and consider ways of keeping our mid-books active and fresh.

1. A good scene is its own complete story arc. Every scene you write has a particular shape and purpose, influenced by motivation, conflict, and resolution. Naturally these will run the range from major to minor, comic to dramatic, mundane to extraordinary and deal with the psychological, emotional, psychical, or physical. But every scene should have its own fulfilled, clear arc—and these arcs are no less important in keeping a reader's attention, and keeping up a book's momentum, than the novel arc as a whole.

2. A good scene informs us about a larger arc. In addition to having its own arc, a good scene also contributes to our understanding of some larger narrative arc or problem. Needing to buy 2% milk, finding out the store only has 1%, and then buying the 1% is itself an arc—it has motivation, conflict, and resolution—but do we understand your

On the Subject

Scene is always necessary to fiction, for it allows readers to see, hear, and sense the story's drama moment-to-moment.

—*Janet Burroway*

detective-protagonist's quest to solve the murder any better because he now owns 1% milk? Well, maybe ... if the detective's interactions inside the store tell us about his state of mind or about his loneliness (perhaps he always buys the pint-sized because he can't go through a half-gallon before it expires).

The purpose of a scene can be to further our understanding of the plot, or of the character, or even to enhance theme or mood, but it has to have *some* reason to exist in the larger context. The most beautiful passage you've ever written that has nothing to do with furthering your story *has to be cut*. This is, again, Faulkner's "killing your darlings," and while it's sometimes tough to do, it's necessary.

3. A good scene has a relationship to what's around it. If you're not sure what the function of a particular scene is—if you're having trouble with tone, pacing, approach, anything—you might find the answer by looking at what's going on in the scenes around it and then playing to or against that. Your scene's reason to exist might be to react to other scenes or anticipate coming ones. Or, a particular scene might exist for the overall pacing of a chapter; two tense scenes in a row might suggest that a third should in some way let the air out, perhaps by introducing levity or humor (if it's called for). Or two light scenes might suggest that the next in some way turn serious, making a point that catches the reader by surprise. If a scene is becoming troublesome, take a step back and consider how it fits in with its neighbors.

4. A good scene is active, focused, and well paced. Is your scene attempting to dump a lot of information on the reader? Is it stretching into long passages of summary? Is it spanning years of backstory in order to make a single, specific point you might make in a much easier, simpler way? These can be the signs of a tired writer—it's much easier to ramble than make sharp choices—so if you find your eyes glossing over what you've written in a scene, scanning whole pages instead of reading, try to figure out what it is you really need to get across in the scene and then look for a smart, focused way of achieving that goal. Simplicity is always harder to achieve than sloppiness, but the simplest way of getting something across is almost always the best. (You might want to look back to the section on pacing on page 147 for some tips on tightening your narrative focus.)

Again, every scene you write is the star of the novel if the reader's staring at it. So no matter what's coming up that you're excited about or hurrying to get to—and no matter how ready you are to get to the end—make sure that each scene you write gets your complete attention and care in the moment.

SUBPLOT SUPPORT

Subplots can be used to good effect in the second act in terms of pacing, allowing the reader to take a break from the main action while offering opportunities to deepen her understanding of the protagonist and his quest. Subplots really come into the text in circular patterns—they announce themselves, set up their own minor arc, and then fall out of the text to reappear later on. You may have to bring many, most, or all of these to completion by the end of the second act, depending upon the needs of your final act and how many of these minor arcs should be resolved before the Climax, or what can be left for the Dénouement (more on this on page 211). In other words, you shouldn't be thinking of these as mere interruptions to the overall story. By the second act you should have an idea of how, and when, these minor arcs play out so that, by mid-book, they're working toward their own conclusions.

It might be helpful to read back through your story and map out all of the subplots you have going—all of the smaller questions you've raised in secondary relationships or story lines that must be resolved in some satisfactory way by the novel's end. Then consider which of these *need* to last until the end of the book and which might be brought to a conclusion somewhere mid-book, so that the final act isn't playing catch-up unnecessarily but is always forward-looking. To that end, see Worksheet 22 on page 256 for help in keeping track of your subplots. If you suddenly realize that you're overloaded with minor subplots, or weighed down by unnecessary ones, take a look at the next section to see how you might get your subplots under control.

OVERACTIVE OR INACTIVE SUBPLOTS

Subplots, as we've said, exist to tell us something about your protagonist and his quest. They're like a side mirror, offering a quick, new (and helpful) perspective and allowing the readers to keep moving forward unimpeded. Thus a subplot becomes problematic when that function breaks down, when it becomes either overactive—trying to take over the main plot and tell its own story instead—or inactive, meaning that it has no clear, compelling connection to the protagonist and the main arc; it's simply there.

An overactive subplot behaves almost like a virus: Its ultimate goal is that it wants to live, like everything else on earth, but in order to do this it invades something healthy, your main plot, and tries to take it over. It might be that the subplot is auditioning for its own novel—it isn't unheard of that a subplot becomes so alive that the author eventually decides to tell that story on its own—but it can't be allowed to take over this one (unless, of course, you come to the realization that the subplot is the plot you actually wanted to explore all along, in which case, well, it's back to the drawing board).

On the Subject

I would never write about anyone who was not at the end of his rope.
—*Stanley Elkin*

An inactive subplot isn't nearly as aggressive; it's not doing anything to take over your novel, or much to advance it, either. In fact it's not doing much except taking up pages and keeping the reader from following the main arc. Most times an inactive subplot exists because the author likes the character of the subplot and has a soft spot for it (even though she probably realizes that there's no reason at all for the subplot to exist). You should ask yourself what the subplot *might* do in the story, why you included it to begin with. If the subplot could have some bearing on the character or main arc, then it might be rehabilitated, making it clear what that relationship is. But if you come to the conclusion that it doesn't really have a bearing on the main action, you have two options: "absorb" it into a preexisting subplot, one that *does* have a reason to be there, or get rid of the subplot altogether.

Again, your subplots are there to further the reader's understanding of the main plot, character, and conflict. But if the relationship between plot and subplot becomes imbalanced, you've got to reestablish the relationship or excise the subplot, as the direction (and fate) of your novel is at stake.

THE DARKEST HOUR

A big trick for you in writing the second act is in navigating the First Culmination, Darkest Moment, and Plot Point 2. Again, the First Culmination is the moment where it seems your protagonist is within reach of his goal yet fails to reach it, leading the character (and reader) to the aptly named Darkest Moment. But your protagonist can't be so beaten in this moment that he simply gives up. In fact, by this point your protagonist must be so invested in the quest, and in the necessity of reaching his goal, that he *can't* simply walk away. Even if you've knocked him down, he has to get up ... because how he pushes toward and faces the final conflict determines the degree to which we identify and sympathize with him.

The First Culmination and Darkest Moment need not be loud, death-defying scenes (though occasionally they can be). Rather, they need be *meaningful*; they must in some way threaten or undermine the character's internal or external quest, or his well-being. And they must be relevant to what the character values and wants, as you've set him up. For example: If your character's external quest is a matter of public or professional record—a cop working on a case, or a social worker trying to rescue a client from a bad situation, or a clergyman trying to protect someone who reached out to him—then casting public or professional aspersion on the protagonist can be just as damning as hitting him over the head with a tire iron, and far more bruising. A deep personal setback can also threaten to derail a protagonist's mission or his life, in the same way personal setbacks sometimes threaten to derail ours, out here in the real world.

Here's a rather sadistic-sounding suggestion for thinking about your own First Culmination and Darkest Moment: What's the absolute worst thing your protagonist might face, the thing he's most fearful of encountering (or, the thing he's most afraid of losing)? If you can have him face it without shutting him down completely, or killing him, then, well … Do it.

How the hero gets back up and keeps going will determine the reader's investment in the third and final act, as the protagonist makes one last push toward achieving the goal. So while I feel sure that you're a very nice person, don't be afraid to make things hard on your character, even to push him to the brink. It will remind the reader of what's at stake in the third act: *Everything's* at stake.

ESCALATING SCENES

The escalating conflicts and building suspense that comprise a strong second act require smart planning—knowing how each individual scene builds to the next, leading to those crucial moments at the end of the act—and smart pacing, so that the middle of the book takes on an inevitable momentum that keeps the reader invested and the hero continually tested and re-tested. To that end, take a look at the worksheets (beginning on page 253) dealing with Act II bridging scenes, subplots, and especially navigating the First Culmination and Darkest Moment and make sure you have a good understanding of those pivotal moments and how they propel protagonist and reader toward the Climax in Act III.

PART TWO
COFFEE BREAK

PLANNING FOR YOUR FINALE

Think back to those classic Saturday morning serials from the 1940s and 50s—with such enviable titles as *Rocket Men From the Moon!*—and to their famous cliffhanger endings, concluding each installment with the hero facing certain doom: the hero's car goes over a cliff, or the plane he was flying blows up in mid-air, etc. The effect of these endings wasn't that the kids in attendance went home depressed because Commander Rick Rocket was blown into pieces that would fit in an ashtray. Instead the effect was a week's worth of bugging their parents to go back *next* Saturday, to see how the hero survived and soldiered on, despite the odds.

That excitement and urgency is very much what you want your *own* readers to feel as they follow your protagonist from the Darkest Moment toward the push he makes in the final act. But while the audiences of those Saturday matinees ultimately expected the hero to succeed, your own readers would be willing to accept either triumph or defeat for the protagonist so long as the ending you offer is fulfilling on its own terms, makes sense in the context of the fictional world you've set up, and is well executed. Consider the following when making your turn toward the final act:

Will the character succeed or fail in reaching his external or internal goals? *Maybe* is not an acceptable answer, though it's possible that the answer to the external and internal questions might not be the same, that the character might meet his external goal but not the personal one, or vice versa. Consider if your protagonist will meet his external and internal goals or not, and then consider what the success or failure of each means for how the reader relates to your story as a whole.

Are you prepared to write the ending your story demands, not the one you personally want it to have? You may've wanted the hero to succeed for as long as you've had the story idea, but does the novel, as you've written it, *earn* and *justify* a happy ending? You should be open to writing the ending that is appropriate to your novel, even if that means considering outcomes you'd never intended.

Are you writing toward an ending that answers your novel's beginning? Go back and look at the questions raised in the book's opening scenes and chapters. In order for your book, and the arcs within, to feel complete, the events at the novel's conclusion must address those earliest questions in satisfying ways. It's the reason the reader has stayed with you and your novel for the duration.

Most of all, write a conclusion that pleases, excites, and satisfies *you*. If you succeed in doing that, chances are you will have done the same for your reader.

PART THREE
ENDINGS

Writing an ending is the most exciting part of a novel project, the culmination of everything you and your characters have been working toward from the start. Included in the final act are those key moments of conflict and resolution you've likely been thinking about since the initial idea caught your attention. The patience and planning that followed, building your book one scene at a time, have finally led you here, to the moment when your character faces the conflict directly and puts everything he's hoped for on the line. There's a reason the reader feels a certain excitement moving toward the end of the book: Because the writer is excited to see how it ends, too.

Even as the pace quickens toward your finale, you should take pains that the work you do in the third and final act is as controlled, purposeful, and artful as the work you've put in throughout, so that both author and reader are rewarded for their investment with a conclusion that's in every way satisfying. To that end, let's consider how the third act functions and what it must achieve by the novel's close.

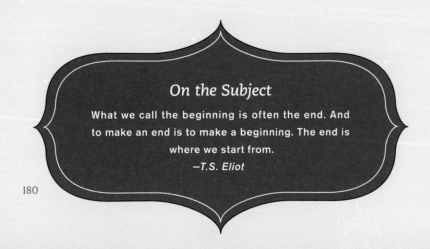

On the Subject

What we call the beginning is often the end. And to make an end is to make a beginning. The end is where we start from.
—*T.S. Eliot*

THE ART OF CLOSING WELL

The momentum of the third act—with the momentum of the entire book behind it—makes the act a whole lot of fun to write, as both author and reader feel propelled toward the final confrontation in the book and the resolution of the story. But in spite of the anticipation you feel to finish the book, it's important to remember that you also have a lot of work to do in the last quarter of your story: fulfill the major plot and character arcs and resolve these in some satisfying way; resolve any outstanding minor arcs of subplot and supporting character, making sure none are left orphaned; build theme from how the resolution of conflict speaks to the broader human experience; and finish with scenes and lines that bring the story to a gratifying conclusion while also encouraging the reader to keep thinking about the characters and their lives even after the book is closed.

Let's consider the art of closing well by first determining the shape and function of a strong final act.

THE SHAPE & FUNCTION OF THE THIRD ACT

In conventional three-act structure, the third act generally accounts for the final 25 percent of the story and includes the Climax, also called the Final Culmination, wherein the protagonist faces the conflict in the most serious, direct way and will either succeed or fail in the overall quest; and the Dénouement, the winding down of action in which the reader takes stock of the protagonist's success or failure and draws conclusions about what the completed arc—and completed story—really means.

Put in these terms, it might seem as if the final act has relatively little to do, but of course that isn't the case: The way your arcs, both major and minor, resolve plays a direct role in what the reader takes away from the book and how she judges it. The reader has made a commitment to see the story through from the beginning, just as the writer has, and she expects a compelling Climax and Dénouement that:

- answer all the questions the book has posed
- reward the anticipation and suspense felt throughout with a final release

On the Subject

Great is the art of beginning, but greater is the art of ending.
—Henry Wadsworth Longfellow

- reveal what the completed arc means for the specific character and his world
- suggest how the completed arc has resonance and meaning for us out here in the real world

Regardless of whether the story ends happily or tragically, the reader expects the story to end well.

But while the way you handle the events at the end of the book—how artfully you tie your story to a close, on a craft level—obviously plays a big role in making meaning, it's important to realize that, if you've set up your story the right way from the beginning and followed through by raising the stakes in incremental, logical ways throughout, keeping the character and his motivation clear, the events themselves in the final act create meaning. A boy who wants ice cream, gets a cone, and then enjoys it on a hot day conveys a specific meaning and feeling to us; a boy who goes through the same steps but then immediately drops the cone onto the hot street, his last dollar in the world melting into the gravel, creates a completely different meaning, a completely different story, just by changing the event waiting for him. The end retroactively affects the way we think about everything that's come before it.

The Climax, then, has to address and jeopardize the character's original external and internal motivations, and the Dénouement has to answer how both of those goals have been met and what the result means for both character and reader. When it's done right, you can look at the end and see reflected back the beginning, or you can flip back to the beginning and see the end. Thus the ending seems on one level inevitable, as if the story couldn't have ended any other way … yet the final outcome hasn't seemed predestined, as the heart of the story contains enough perilous conflict that the character's success is never a foregone conclusion. The success of the character in his quest—and the success of the story as a whole—has to be earned along the way.

Let's run our three examples through one last time to see how they meet up with the shape and function of a third act.

THE WIZARD OF OZ

Climax / Final Culmination moment of direct conflict for the character, with everything he's hoped for at stake	Dénouement the winding down that reveals how the story has come full circle	Result what the character and reader are left with
The Wizard of Oz gets quite greedy in its third act, offering several moments that seem to be the final culmination but that, even when resolved, fail to get Dorothy to her goal, forcing a next round of conflict: Dorothy and friends face off with the Witch, destroy her, and get her broom (which doesn't get Dorothy home); they take the broomstick to the Wizard, who then tries to scare them off, forcing conflict with him (he's defeated when Toto reveals him to be just a man behind a curtain); the Wizard promises to take Dorothy back to Kansas via hot-air balloon … which then, through circumstance, takes off without her, making it seem that Dorothy has failed in the quest; and	Dorothy wakes up in Kansas with her family and their farmhands around her, all of whom good-naturedly dismiss her story of Oz, though Dorothy is sure that it all happened. More importantly, she knows for sure what she didn't know at the beginning of the story: that this place is her home.	**External motivation or goal met:** Dorothy finds a way back to Kansas. **Internal motivation or goal met:** Dorothy realizes that her aunt and uncle's farm is where she really belongs.

finally it's Glinda the Good Witch who reveals that all Dorothy has to do to get home is click her heels (thanks for the info there, Glinda). This third act, in other words, behaves almost like a higher-octane version of the second act, continually putting up obstacles and delaying Dorothy's success. (By comparison, the Dénouement is very, very quick.)

NOTE: Again, this really follows the film version, which is obliged to sustain conflict and raise the final stakes in much more dramatic ways, appropriate for a much larger and more sophisticated audience, than the children's book.

THE SILENCE OF THE LAMBS

Climax / Final Culmination	Dénouement	Result
moment of direct conflict for the character, with everything he's hoped for at stake	the winding down that reveals how the story has come full circle	what the character and reader are left with
Unlike *The Wizard of Oz*, which keeps raising tension toward the final culmination by introducing an escalating series of new conflicts, the climax	Starling, having saved Catherine Martin and stopped a serial killer, graduates from the FBI academy and is made an agent. Both her arc as a	**External motivation or goal met:** Starling saves Catherine Martin's life and ends Buffalo Bill's killing spree.

of *The Silence of the Lambs* is straightforward and direct: Clarice Starling, realizing that she's stumbled upon the killer, has to face Jame Gumm on his own turf, alone.

But it's certainly no less tense; Harris raises the stakes by having Starling, the young trainee, follow Gumm down the stairs to his basement like descending into Hell. Gumm knows precisely where he is, not just because it's his horror house but because he's prepared, wearing night-vision goggles, cutting the lights. Starling, on the other hand, is completely ill-prepared on almost every level, but she has no choice: she has to follow him downstairs and face him in order to save Catherine Martin. Which, after several dark and very tense pages down in the basement, she does.

The Wizard of Oz crafts third-act Climax by going ever-bigger; Harris does it by going smaller, more focused, more confined, and, because of this, more terrifying.

character and the larger plot arc are fulfilled.

But Harris famously leaves the audience with one last tease—toward the end of the second act, Lecter escapes his captors. In the book's final chapter we have Lecter, on the loose and enjoying a fine wine, writing Starling a note to wish her well, assure her he has no plans to "call on" her, and asking her for the same courtesy. Thus the reader closes the book wondering what might happen next ... a question it would take Harris twenty years to answer in his follow-up.

Internal motivation or goal met:

Starling has proven herself beyond what she, or anyone else, would've thought, facing down not just her demons but even the threat of death and prevailing, and her efforts are rewarded with validation and self-validation. As the text tells us, "She was healing."

THE LORD OF THE RINGS: THE FELLOWSHIP OF THE RING

Climax / Final Culmination	Dénouement	Result
moment of direct conflict for the character, with everything he's hoped for at stake	the winding down that reveals how the story has come full circle	what the character and reader are left with
The Fellowship leaves Lothlórien for Mordor, but the Fellowship, already coming apart, is finally destroyed when one of its members, Boromir, tries to take the Ring from Frodo. Realizing that the seduction of the Ring makes it impossible to trust others (and puts others at risk), Frodo decides to leave the Fellowship and make the rest of the journey alone. As his companions ready themselves for a confrontation with approaching Orcs, Frodo slips away, accompanied only by his friend Sam, who refuses to let Frodo go it alone.	The Dénouement of *The Fellowship of the Ring* foreshadows the conflicts to come in the next book and reveals a far different, far wiser Frodo than the one who began the book. The One Ring is too powerful, and as a result Frodo has to bear its responsibility on his own. He realizes that he is, for the most part, alone … but all of this is accomplished quickly. The conflict and Dénouement both hinge on Frodo's decision to go alone, leaving us in a state of anticipation and tension for the next book.	**External motivation or goal met:** Not yet–though certainly the circumstances have changed dramatically over the course of the book. **Internal motivation or goal met:** Not yet–though, as we just saw, Frodo as a character has indeed completed an arc, and a rather depressing one. He'd hoped to have help in accomplishing the monumental task ahead of him, and in the beginning and middle of the book that looked possible. But the result of the Final Culmination–a member of the Fellowship turning on him to acquire the Ring–is that Frodo has matured, become more pragmatic, possibly less trusting, which the Ring will play, and prey, upon in the books to come.

		The larger arc of *LOTR* hasn't yet been met, but we certainly recognize the arc of the first install-ment on its own. And the ultimate result, fortunately for Tolkien, is that we want to pick up the next and see how the story plays out.

ACCOUNTING FOR
THE UNACCOUNTABLE

This may be strange to hear, since your finale is something you've likely known from the very beginning, but it's not uncommon for an author to have an ending in mind from the start that he realizes, by the end, needs to change. This might be the result of your characters growing and evolving over the course of the novel, or of subtle changes in plot that have altered the course of the book, or any number of events that have taken the story places you didn't anticipate. This isn't a reason to panic; no writer, no matter how meticulous in her planning, writes the book she intended to at the outset. Novel writing, as we've said a number of times, is as much about discovery as it is planning. You should be much more worried if *nothing* surprised you along the way.

Nevertheless, because our ending scenes tend to come to us so early in the process, and stay so vivid in our imaginations, it can be difficult to allow them the freedom to change and grow; we become attached to them to the point where we'll force them into the story if we have to (probably because we're afraid that, if we don't end up where we originally intended, we've done something wrong).

This isn't the time to psych yourself out. If your third act has a momentum of its own and is pushing you toward a conclusion, even if that conclusion is one you never planned, write it. See where it wants to go. The most important thing you can do at this point is finish a draft of your book and see it through; there will be plenty of time to make all your happy accidents look purposeful in the revision process (see page 216). Besides, many of the best novel endings you've ever read were crafted this same way, by getting something down, seeing what the novel was trying to do, and then rewriting until the whole thing seemed to come out perfect the first time. Welcome the happy accident, even when it runs counter to what you wish the book would do. There's a good chance that the story is right.

THE ROLE OF THEME

Theme is the ultimate unifying force in a novel, connecting the character's external quest to the internal one, revealing how the actions and events in the book are all interrelated, and providing the reader a way to personally connect with the story, to see aspects of herself and her own experiences in the characters'. If we were looking to formulate a rather simple definition of theme, we might say this: Theme is the big-picture meaning of a work, related closely to the events in the work, which shows how the characters' personal plight relates to, and is part of, the larger human experience.

Before we go on with our discussion, let's make sure we really understand what we mean by this, looking at an example I've used before with my students. If I asked you to tell me what *Forrest Gump*—novel or film, take your pick—is about on a plot level, in just a sentence, how would you answer? You'd probably say something like, "It's the story of a mentally challenged man who nevertheless goes on to live an extraordinary life." Okay, sounds good.

Now, if I asked you to extrapolate from that one-sentence summary the work's theme, the basic understanding about the human experience that we take away from it, what would you say? Maybe something along the lines of: "Even the

On the Subject

Fiction is a piece of truth that turns lies to meaning.
—*Dorothy Allison*

simplest person can live an extraordinary life." We might even tweak this a little bit to explain what we mean by "extraordinary life." Forrest Gump, after all, doesn't just live well but seems to be present at, even occasionally has a direct influence on, the major events that shaped the American twentieth century. (He taught Elvis how to dance, for cryin' out loud.) So we might want our stated theme to indicate this somehow, as in: "Even the simplest person can have an extraordinary impact on the world."

We've really arrived at theme pretty easily by considering what the character's individual story means for us out here in the real world. And if you look back at the events in the story—from Forrest's brief encounters with the famous (or infamous) to his service in Vietnam to his personal relationships to, well, name it—you see that all the events, no matter how seemingly disparate from one another, are really aspects of the same thing, making the point in different ways. The theme unifies the work.

You might be asking yourself, "If theme's so important in holding a novel together, then why are we just talking about it now, at the end of the story?" Good question. I'm glad you asked.

When we start out intending to write toward a certain theme— when we say, "I'm going to write a novel about how even the simplest person can have a big impact on the world"—what we're likely to end up with is didacticism, a bit of old-time preaching, rather than a novel. Theme and moral sometimes get used interchangeably even by people who know better, but there's a big difference between the two: a moral, such as we see in fairy tales, intends to teach us a lesson, to tell us how to live. Theme, on the other hand, doesn't tell us how to live but reveals something about the way we live, allows us to look at our lives differently. Consciously writing toward theme from the beginning sets us up to moralize, to tell others how to go about their lives, which is obviously not something the novel can, or should, do. But when we start out with a clear character, with clear wants and limitations, and begin putting him in situations that test him as a person, we begin to see theme naturally emerge from the chain of events as a result of our curiosity and questioning as novelists. We don't write to show others what we know, like a tent-revivalist or propagandist, but to test what we know and see if our ideas hold up or are disproven. This is how we find our way into the story, how we fit in as authors even as we write. It's also how the reader finds her way into the story and connects with it. And both have to do with the creation of theme, the meaning that is both specific to your characters in their situations and yet applicable to us in ours.

The proper time to think about theme in your novel is now, as you begin wrapping up your story and are able to draw conclusions about it in the context of the larger world. As you begin to see theme emerge, you'll be able to go back and more consciously direct the novel toward it in the process of revision, streamlining the story so that the events that take place lead the reader toward thematic meaning.

Take a look at the following exercise, designed to get you thinking about the bigger theme suggested by, and present within, your novel.

EXERCISE: FINDING YOUR THEME

Directions: For each story listed below—and your own personal favorites—construct a broad, one-sentence summary of the work and try to draw from that a one-sentence statement of the novel's theme. Then, craft a one-sentence summary of your *own* novel and draw out theme in the same way.

Novel: *Forrest Gump*

Summary: A mentally-challenged man lives an extraordinary life and helps shape the course of a century.

Theme: Even the simplest person can have an extraordinary impact on the world.

Novel: *Moby-Dick*
    Summary:
    Theme:
Novel (your choice):
    Summary:
    Theme:
Novel (your choice):
    Summary:
    Theme:
Your novel:
    Summary:
    Theme:

SKETCHING AN ENDING

Turn to Worksheet 25: The Shape of the Third Act on page 259 and sketch out your own important final-act moments, using the earlier examples from this section as a guide. Again, you'll want to consider not just where and how your story ends, on a basic plot level, but what the effect of the ending will be on the reader, how the conclusion of the character's internal and external arcs will resonate with the reader on a personal level and suggest larger theme.

Keep in mind that you're not bound by the sketch you make and that you should, in fact, be open to the unaccountable if your story starts leading you to a conclusion you didn't necessarily intend; remember, the most surprising ending you'll encounter in a novel is likely one that took the author by surprise, too. For more on navigating the Climax and Dénouement of your novel—and in differentiating effective and ineffective surprise in a finale—turn to the next section, Plotting for the Payoff.

THE NIGHTTIME NOVELIST

PLOTTING FOR THE PAYOFF

Every novel has its own particular needs in plotting a payoff. Take a quick look back at the third acts we sketched, beginning on page 184, using our three faithful examples, and you'll see what I mean: *The Wizard of Oz* delays the Climax several times by putting new obstacles in Dorothy's way, and the Dénouement is pretty quick, with all subplots resolved by the time Dorothy clicks her heels. *The Silence of the Lambs*, on the other hand, moves straight from Plot Point 2 to the tense Climax, leaving room to tie up loose threads and subplots in the much quieter Dénouement (except for one major subplot neatly unresolved: Lecter on the loose). Finally, *The Fellowship of the Ring*'s Climax and Dénouement come very quickly, back to back, in the final chapter of the book, in the moment Frodo decides to make the rest of the journey alone. As a result, the tension is never really broken but continues until the reader picks up the next book.

Just as the endings of these three books are unique in how they approach third-act plotting, your novel will have its own specific needs; it would be impossible to tell you, for example, "Your Climax should be ten pages" or "Your Dénouement should be twenty." Really, the only thing that can dictate the plotting and pacing of the end is what's come before it—what expectations you've raised and have to meet—in the last act.

Still, there are a number of things you might take into account in order to figure out how to best pull off the payoff.

THE BIG CLIMAX

Thinking about your third-act events and how you anticipate the act playing out, try answering the following questions:

1. How close to the end of the book is the Climax? Both *The Wizard of Oz* and *The Fellowship of the Ring* delay the Climax—the first through action following Plot Point 2, the second through exposition—until very late, with little Dénouement even necessary. *The Silence of the Lambs*, on the other hand, arrives at the Climax quickly after Plot Point 2 and then spends pages winding down, tying up subplots, filling in the blanks, checking in on Starling (and then Lecter), and so on. Consider what your climactic moment is, how quickly you get there from Plot Point 2, and how much you'll really need to linger in the Dénouement.

2. When should you tie up your subplots? When your Climax comes very late in the book, you'll need to make sure that your subplots are brought to a close by the time you arrive there (unless the Climax sufficiently ties them up). If, on the other hand, your Climax requires

On the Subject

Plot is the aesthetic approximation of gravity.
—*Joyce Carol Oates*

necessary winding down—if, for example, you're writing a detective story, which necessitates a bit of post-mortem—then you'll need to reach the Climax quickly enough to allow for a longer Dénouement. (NOTE: As mentioned on page 174, it's often appropriate to tie up your minor subplots, the ones that have no direct bearing on the finale, before the Climax so the reader's attention will be focused on the right thing.)

3. Does your Climax leave more questions than answers? If you find yourself with too much left to explain after the Climax, especially as a result of the Climax (rather than just necessary Dénouement), are you trying to do too much too late? Have you created a complex climactic scene when a more straightforward one might do? Your ending should become more and more focused up to your climactic moment and should then wind down simply, in ways that resolve complication easily (your reader is likely a bit exhausted after the Climax and can't take on too much responsibility). So if you've still got large knots to untie at the end, try to find ways to simplify the third act—even if it means going back to your first and second acts to simplify them, too.

TWIST YOUR ENDING, NOT A KNIFE IN THE READER'S BACK

On page 129, we discussed the effective use of suspense in fiction, particularly in crafting a second act. Now, as we think about constructing a strong ending, it behooves us to consider effective—and ineffective—uses of surprise.

Surprises in plot, especially "twist" endings, operate in a very specific way: They catch us off guard in the moment, but in retrospect they appear to have been unavoidable, set up and even suggested by what we've already seen. Consider, for instance, the twist ending we see in O. Henry's classic short story "The Gift of the Magi" in which a young married couple without much money struggles to buy Christmas gifts for one another. The young wife, Della, wants to buy a gold chain for her husband, Jim, for his prized pocket watch, but she is well short of the money it would cost. So Della decides to trade in the one thing she has of value—her long hair, which she cuts off and sells to a wig-maker—in order to buy the chain. When Jim comes home that evening, he stops short and stares at his newly shorn wife with a "peculiar expression" that Della believes is dislike for her new haircut, and she immediately tells him that it will grow back, not to be concerned, that she has a wonderful Christmas gift for

On the Subject

I hate tricks. At the first sign of a trick or a gimmick in a piece of fiction, a cheap trick or even an elaborate trick, I tend to duck for cover.
—*Raymond Carver*

him. It's then that O. Henry reveals the reason for the peculiar expression: Jim has sold his pocket watch for the money to buy his wife a Christmas gift she'd love: combs for her beautiful long hair. The twist is delightful, moving, but it's also an inevitable conclusion. The surprise catches us off guard for just a moment, feels strangely euphoric, but in the very next moment the surprise makes complete sense: We realize we've been headed toward that conclusion all along.

Think of your own favorite example of a successful twist ending—whether in the O. Henry example above, or the *Twilight Zone* episode in which Burgess Meredith plays the book lover who survives an apocalypse and finally has time to read, and then immediately breaks his glasses, or the end of *The Sixth Sense* where we find out that Bruce Willis is [spoiler deleted]—and see if it doesn't operate the same way. The surprise works because, once we look back on it, we realize we should've seen it coming, though we're thankful we didn't. The twist is part of a logical progression.

Ineffective surprise, on the other hand, is apropos absolutely nothing, comes out of nowhere, has no reason to be there, and in fact often runs counter to what we'd been led to believe. And the effect on the reader is momentary surprise, and then any number of emotions you absolutely don't want to evoke in your audience, ever, at least if they're directed back at you: confusion, anger, disgust, betrayal, rage, demands for a refund … .

Here is a brief listing of the most common trick-ending offenders, the ones that don't delight the reader so much as insult and offend him. Be careful not to fall back on any of these—not because they can't be used effectively, but because they rarely are.

- *The deus ex machina.* The literal translation, "god from the machine," has an even more literal origin: In Greek tragedy, when playwrights had worked their characters into such a mess that there seemed no real way to resolve the crisis, someone would lower a god onto the stage via a machine, like a wench, so the god could solve the problem with his godly powers and then be wenched back off stage. In contemporary usage it refers to any resolution that involves introducing some external solution to the problem from out of nowhere, such as saying, "And then he saw the lifeboat!" or "And then he saw the machine gun!" or "And then he saw the UFO!" where no lifeboat, machine gun, or UFO existed in the story before. There's always a way to solve a story dilemma using what's already been introduced into the story. And in those rare occasions when there's not, then maybe you shouldn't be getting your characters into such a complicated mess, huh?

- *The rule-changer.* At the beginning of every novel, the author sets the rules for the story and its fictional world, the reader agrees, and thus author and reader form a kind of contract. If at the end of the story you suddenly begin changing those rules—in the process chiding the reader for being such a dope as to believe you in the first place—the reader feels cheated, because she has been. Examples of this include such endings as It Was All A Dream/ Hallucination/Virtual-reality Experiment or anything else that indicates the contract the reader trusted at the beginning of the story should never have been.

- *The (very) delayed reveal.* When a twist comes from the author delaying the reveal of certain crucial information—withheld for the purposes of deceiving the reader—the reader reaction is naturally one of betrayal. Examples of this include stories that, in the last line, reveal that the main character is acting so odd because he's actually a dog (or a Martian, or a ghost, or a time-traveling Nazi, or whatever) when that information should've been made part of the rules of the story up front.

All of these run the risk of alienating a reader, so the best rule to follow is not to resort to them at all. Rather, allow surprise to come naturally from the directions your story takes. Don't try to manufacture or force surprise, at the end or anywhere else.

CHECKING FOR PLOT HOLES

There's a famous story that illustrates how even masterful storytellers can end up with glaring holes in their plots. It concerns Raymond Chandler's classic detective novel *The Big Sleep* in which the killing of a chauffeur helps launch a series of complex mysteries involving drugs, pornography, blackmail, and murder that Chandler's hero, Phillip Marlowe, must solve. When the novel was later made into an equally classic film starring Humphrey Bogart as Marlowe—with a screenplay by William Faulkner—the crew realized during production that there was one last question to resolve: Who killed the chauffeur? As the story goes, director Howard Hawks first called Faulkner wanting to know, who had no idea, so Hawks wired Chandler, the source, and asked him who killed the chauffeur. Chandler's response, as he later recalled, was to-the-point: "Dammit, I didn't know either."

To make sure your plot is as solid as it can be—before some legendary film director discovers a plot hole while trying to adapt your work—consider the following questions and see that you have them answered in your novel.

On the Subject

In one place in *Deerslayer*, and in the restricted space of two-thirds of a page, [James Fenimore] Cooper has scored 114 offenses against literary art out of a possible 115. It breaks the record.
—*Mark Twain*

- *Have all subplots and supporting character arcs been concluded?* You might want to go back through the novel and mark those moments with subplot and supporting cast that seem to demand revisiting later ... and make sure you did revisit and conclude them in some satisfying way.

- *Do you find any of your characters indulging in excessive monologue toward the finale?* Late-novel monologues often indicate that certain information should have been introduced earlier but wasn't—and now your character is trying to catch the reader up on that omitted information in one big breath. These one-breath wonders suggest a hole in the plot that the character is now trying to plug, poorly. Be aware of any such information dumps you come across, and consider how you might plug the hole yourself earlier in the text.

- *Do the events in your novel follow the rules of the story as you've set them out?* We already discussed rule breaking in terms of the "twist" ending, but the same applies to every turn your story takes. If your protagonist is launched on his adventure when he saves a young woman from drowning, but then at Plot Point 1 he lets the antagonist get away because he's not a very strong swimmer, that's obviously a problem, and everything that comes after that point will be looked on with suspicion by the reader (if he's still reading at all).

- *Do the events in your novel follow, and account for, the rules of logic?* If it's revealed at the end of your novel that your time-traveling hero has fallen in love with his own grandmother and is now his own grandfather, your reader will likely either scratch his head or kick your novel across the room, depending on what kind of day he's having. It's absolutely true that, as an author, you control the powers of time and space in your book—see the section on pacing on page 147—but even so you're still bound by the general rules of logic; what you do has to make sense. Thus anything that doesn't seem possible, or at least believable, is a problem you'll need to fix.

Sometimes we get so caught up in the momentum of our story, in the fun of telling it, that we forget to properly account for, explain, or excise inconsistencies along the way; even Raymond Chandler can let a dead chauffeur slip past him. But the smallest plot hole might still be big enough for your reader to fall straight through, so be mindful that your plot be as solid as it can be. And if there's anything in the story you can't reconcile, you may want to consider what the offending element is doing there in the first place.

THE READER PAYOFF (PART I)

The Climax of the novel answers one of the story's two major questions: Will the protagonist succeed or fail in meeting his external goal? (The second big question, addressed in the Dénouement, is what the success or failure means for the character as a person, which affects how we relate to the character at the end.) In order for the Climax to feel truly like a payoff, it must answer the external question one way or the other—either with success or failure—and it has to seem like a natural, believable conclusion, even if the end holds a surprise or two for the reader.

Keep in mind, though, that while success or failure are indeed your only two options in concluding the protagonist's external arc, the effect of either one can produce complex meaning for protagonist and reader alike. A failure in the external quest doesn't necessarily mean failure for the character's internal quest, and vice versa. Thus a failure of the external quest might still lead to a triumphant ending in terms of the internal, and a success in the external might be bittersweet if the internal goal is nevertheless unmet. (Don't believe me? Go watch the end of *Casablanca* and then give me a call.)

When writing your climactic scenes, then, go back to your first act—to the point where the internal and external goals became parallel and launched the hero, and the reader, on the journey—and consider how your Climax, whether win or lose for the main character, answers the questions posed at the book's beginning. And you should also consider how either a win or loss in the Climax affects what you're able to do in the book's Dénouement, where the reader can begin taking stock of everything that's transpired along the way (and how your main character has been changed by the experience).

CONSIDERING THE CLIMAX

The Climax is the greatest point of tension and conflict in the novel, and how that conflict plays out, how the tension resolves, is part of the payoff the reader has been waiting for since the beginning, allowing her to see the story as a full arc and to draw conclusions about the character's journey. To that end, you'll want to consider not just how your own Climax will resolve—with the character either succeeding or failing in the external quest—but what the implications are in terms of the larger story, leading to the Dénouement and resonant closing scenes of the book.

Take a look at Worksheet 26: Climax on page 260 and consider how your own Climax fulfills the external arc, bringing that part of the journey to a satisfying close, while also leading your reader toward the Dénouement, where the effect of the win or loss on the protagonist's personal or internal quest will be revealed.

COMING FULL CIRCLE

If the Climax answers the *primary* question of the book, which is to say, whether the character succeeds or fails in reaching the overall external goal, the Dénouement puts the victory or failure into perspective, showing its effect on the protagonist and his relationship to the world. This gives the reader a way of knowing what to take away from the story.

The closing moments are necessarily quieter than the climactic scene, but they should be no less emotionally resonant; in fact, the Dénouement is a moment that looks back to, and reminds the reader of, the beginning of your novel and what questions were raised there, particularly in terms of the protagonist's internal motivation. What your character wants personally has been driving the narrative since the first page, even before the external motivation and conflict came along to parallel the personal struggle. With the external question resolved in the Climax, what remains is answering the internal question and addressing the effect the story has had on the character as a person, thus bringing the character arc, and the book, full circle.

On the Subject

It will turn out that your first page has a lot to do
with your last page.
—*Doris Betts*

THE COMPLETED CHARACTER ARC

One of the most basic definitions of a story—in fact a common test to determine if what you have is *truly* a story rather than, say, an anecdote or a yarn or some other related form—is that it's a complete action that leaves the protagonist in some way changed by the experience. For example, look back to *The Fellowship of the Ring*, which we discussed in the section on third-act arc on page 187. As part of a trilogy, the book really doesn't fulfill the overall arc set up at the beginning; for that, we'll need to follow the story for two more installments. Yet *The Fellowship of the Ring* is clearly a complete story on its own—no one left the theater demanding their money back because Frodo didn't make it to Mordor in three hours—because the protagonist has indeed fulfilled an arc; just compare Frodo at the beginning of the book to the version we see at the end. We know it's a complete story because the events have had a clear, discernable effect on the protagonist. He is not the same person.

The reader will put *your* book to this test, too; your protagonist has to be in some way altered by the experience in order for the story to feel complete. Now, this doesn't mean that your protagonist needs to succeed, necessarily, nor does it mean that he needs to be better, smarter, or more excellent than he was at the beginning; in fact, failure—particularly our own personal failings—often change our lives with more ferocity than our successes. But however the events unfold, and no matter where they leave our protagonist, the effect must be *significant* for the character. The way to gauge the significance is by looking at the protagonist at both the beginning and end and seeing a difference. If the character seems unchanged by the end of the story, it must be because the events he went through weren't really that important. (And if the events weren't really that important, why did the reader just spend all that time, energy, and attention *reading* them?)

So here's the big question to put to your own work: Has the protagonist met both his external and internal goals by the end of the novel? The correct answer is either a yes or a no; there's no *maybe*. And that yes or no, that success or failure, should finally give the reader a full understanding of both the character and story. The reader should feel the personal victory or loss as if it were her own.

THE UNCHANGED PROTAGONIST

If, on the other hand, you begin to see that your protagonist is essentially static and unchanging in the final act and in the book as a whole—and especially if your protagonist has neither succeeded or failed in the quest but has arrived at some kind of ambiguous middle ground—that's a big problem. It's not necessarily one that negates all your hard work to this point, but it's *absolutely* one you'll need to reconcile in revision by refocusing the work so that the protagonist's arc is central to what happens. To get started, ask yourself these questions about your story and protagonist:

1. Is your protagonist's motivation evident at the beginning of your novel?

2. Is it clear what would be personally at stake for the protagonist if he fails?

3. Does your protagonist's motivation stay consistent throughout the novel?

On the Subject

The test of a round character is whether it is capable of surprising in a convincing way.
—*E.M. Forster*

4. Does your protagonist have one, and only one, clear internal motivation that you could state very simply?
5. Do the events in the novel have a clear relationship back to what the character wants and what's at risk?
6. Is there something concrete keeping your protagonist from simply walking away in the book, some personal reason he *has* to see the story through?

At the point where any of these prompts a "no," then at least you know the start of your problem, though resolving it might mean some hard work, depending upon how far off course the novel has veered as a result. And if you're still having trouble connecting with your protagonist as a person, ask yourself: How would *I* react if I were in the same situation? What would *I* be concerned with, or afraid of, when facing down this problem? How would my concerns or fears affect my actions? And, especially, consider this: If I failed, how much would I lose? How much would my life change? What would I never get back?

Of course your protagonist likely will have *several* things at stake as your novel progresses, ranging from the personal and emotional to the public or professional up to your protagonist's way of life or even his *very* life. But as stakes rise, you should have *more* of an understanding of why the events are significant to him, not less. And the threat of what your protagonist might lose shows you the effect of what he'll win, why he's a different person at the end of your story than at the beginning. Find how you personally connect with the character, how you would feel considering the stakes, and then explore his humanity honestly; you'll find your reader connecting with your character and his arc, too.

DÉNOUEMENT & CRAFTING CLOSING SCENES

The term *dénouement* comes from the French (and earlier Latin) for "untying," as you would a knot—for instance, all those knots of plot, character, and conflict you've spent your novel making. Interestingly, though, when I teach Dénouement I find I'm actually using the term in an opposite way from its literal meaning: Dénouement is about *tying up* those necessary loose threads and making sure they are woven back into the novel in some meaningful way by the end. The Dénouement is about completion.

The needs of your particular genre will affect what you cover in the Dénouement and how you cover it. A detective story or procedural, for example, might require a bit of post-mortem (perhaps literally) after the Climax, revealing those last pieces of information that only make sense now that the mystery has been solved, whereas a fantasy might require very little after the Climax for us to understand the overall meaning: good defeated evil, and that's all you need to know. In a love story, what we need is some understanding of what the climactic moment ultimately means for the lovers, whether they'll live happily ever after or not. But it's important for you to remember that the Dénouement isn't about offering information only; the artistry with which you answer these remaining questions, and the mood your strike with your closing lines, goes a long way to informing the reader how to interpret the end.

Here's a quick, beautiful example from Charles Dickens's *Great Expectations*. The plot of the book concerns Pip, a boy of humble means who receives money—and thus an opportunity to better himself socially and become a "gentleman"—from a mysterious benefactor. The major (external) question of the book, then, is about Pip's making his way in the larger world, which takes too many Dickensian twists and turns along the way to name. But the major subplot—and the emotional heart of the book—has to do with Pip's longing for the young Estella, the ward of the eccentric Miss Havisham. Pip and Estella's relationship over the many years (thirty-plus) covered in the novel is turbulent, with Estella toying with Pip at the urging of Miss Havisham and breaking his heart repeatedly, eventually by marrying another—though the reader never truly gives up hope that Pip might find happiness with her (since this is something Pip desperately wants, and we want what Pip wants). At the end of the novel, Pip—having by this time earned, lost, and begun rebuilding his fortune—returns to his boyhood home and to the crumbling ruins of Miss Havisham's home, where he finds, of all people, Estella, whose marriage is done and who seems genuinely sorry for having treated Pip so poorly.

The last lines of the novel are a classic example of how Dénouement artfully ties up the action of the story while offering a bit of understanding—and hope—for what comes next:

> I took her hand in mine, and we went out of the ruined place; and, as the morning mists had risen long ago when I first left the forge, so, the evening mists were rising now, and in all the broad expanse of tranquil light they showed to me, I saw no shadow of another parting from her.

Pip has achieved the major external goal of the book—he has become a man of means, and self-sufficient in the process—though the reader turns toward the last chapter still wondering about that major unresolved subplot, and meaningful goal, of finding a measure of love and happiness. The way Dickens addresses these in the Dénouement, and offers hope that Pip has finally found what he's looking for, is the perfect, satisfying conclusion we've been waiting for, and it's achieved through a rather simple and even understated image: Pip and Estella holding hands, not letting go.

THE READER PAYOFF (PART II)

Great opening lines tend to get a good bit of attention and discussion from readers—and for good reason, as we've discussed the necessity of a compelling opening hook—but the closing pages and last lines of a novel are every bit as important. Think back to the last time you read a book that ended so artfully you closed the book and spent the next ten minutes in a kind of reverie … still in the world of the novel, still thinking about the characters and their lives, even though their journey had come to a close. And you were likely thinking about what the characters' journey meant for your *own* life: how the struggle depicted in the book in some way resonated with you and made you think of your own journey in a different way.

Ending where the story began, with internal motivation, gives the reader a sense of emotional satisfaction and the book its sense of symmetry and completion. Importantly, it allows all involved a clear way of gauging what's really been accomplished in the story. By showing the effect of the victory or loss on the character as a person, how the character has been altered by the experience, we help the reader understand the full implication of the character's quest, why the journey has been meaningful for the protagonist and the reader. And when this is done as artfully as in the Dickens example on page 212, the Dénouement and closing scenes encourage the reader to keep thinking about the characters and their lives even after the book is finished.

When considering your own Dénouement and the reader payoff it brings, look back to the protagonist's internal motivation at the beginning of the book and find a satisfying way to resolve that personal quest by tying up loose threads, by answering the internal question in a clear, right way, but also in terms of the line-by-line pleasures of the text. Strive for that line or image that'll announce itself as the rightful, and the only possible, end of the journey.

ENDING WITH THE BEGINNING

You're within shouting distance of having finished the novel, and the most important thing you can do to see the book through is to remind yourself of how you got here, looking back at the beginning, remembering what it is that you're really moving toward, what needs to be fulfilled (and, importantly, what you should do in the final act to make the book as a whole fulfilling).

You shouldn't get so concerned about any dangling or orphaned plot points, about polishing, that you find yourself trying to play it too safe. By all means, if you've made it this far you deserve to let go a bit and have fun. (Besides, there will be plenty of opportunity in the next phase, revision, to make your final draft look as if it came out perfect the first time.) But try to think of the momentum and urgency of the final act as coming from the first two acts and what you set up there. In the end is the beginning, and you'll know you've *really* finished the novel when that initial question, raised by that very first spark, has found a resonant, satisfying conclusion.

For some help in crafting a compelling close—and considering what you'll need to cover in your final moments—see Worksheet 27: Dénouement & Closing Scenes on page 261. But keep in mind that ending well means more than just offering the right information; it's about finding that inspired way of conveying meaning and emotion to the reader so that she wants to inhabit the world you've created even after the reading is done.

REVISION: DISCOVERING WHAT YOU MEANT

A first draft requires a fine balance of intelligence, intuition, perseverance, and—if you're lucky—luck. Finishing a novel draft is a rightful accomplishment; and if you're at this point now, with a draft done, then put it down for a few days, go out and celebrate, rejoin the world, see a movie, catch up on some sleep, and enjoy a victory lap. Then, once you've let your manuscript sit for a few days, pick it back up and read it through. What you'll find are passages you don't even remember writing, some of them heartbreaking, mysterious, wonderful. Some of your scenes will seem so alive they pop right off the page. Some of your turns in plot and character, as well as your turns of phrase, will catch you by surprise, despite the fact you wrote them. You're going to find some very good stuff in those pages.

But make no mistake: You will also find a whole lot wrong. You'll find narration and characterization and dialogue and plotting that are, you now realize, not just weak (which you would actually welcome)

On the Subject

Writing and rewriting are a constant search for what one is saying.
—*John Updike*

but among the worst atrocities ever committed by pen against poor innocent paper. If there are moments reading over the draft that make you want to call a friend to read a passage over the phone, there will be just as many that make you thankful that writing is solitary work, that nobody was there to witness how bad it gets.

Good. Great. Perfect.

This is one of the most important esoteric secrets you'll learn in the course of your initiation as a novelist: All novels begin as clumsy first drafts that find their focus, cohesion, and eventual perfection—or close as we can get—through the process of revision. Sometimes that process takes a couple of drafts, and sometimes it takes a couple of *years*, but it's important that we give revision its due—whatever it requires. Revision is too often considered synonymous with straight-up editing, with tedious left-brain chore-work, when in fact it's a process of discovery every bit as important, and often as inspiring, as the writing itself. It's an opportunity to see patterns emerge you hadn't intended or foreseen, to watch your characters assert themselves as human beings, to uncover a larger theme in the work but also smaller motifs suggesting meaning you're surprised to find there. Seeing what you said is an important step in seeing what you really *meant* to say, and the more conscious steering of the work toward a unified whole comes now, as you rewrite the novel so that it seems, to the reader, that the story emerged perfectly, and almost without effort, the first time around.

Let's approach our discussion of revision in the same way you'll approach it in your book, looking first at the big picture so we'll know how to manage the smaller word-by-word changes to come.

REVISING THE MACRO: LETTING THE STORY LEAD

What I'm about to say will probably sound strange at first, given all the time we've spent discussing how to consciously craft and direct your story, but it still has the virtue of being true: It's not really about what *you* want for your story, when it comes right down to it. It's about what the story wants to be.

Revision offers you an opportunity, as the term suggests, to see your story in a new way, though what you end up seeing might be different from what you'd *intended*—you'd set out to write a light-hearted comedy, for instance, and yet here's this darker thread that surprises you on a read-through. But just because you didn't intend it doesn't mean it shouldn't be there. This is part of the mystery of writing, and the artistic process in general: The subconscious inevitably begins to infiltrate and influence the conscious design, steering the work in subtle but important new ways. In other words, the story begins telling you things you didn't necessarily know about it, telling you what it wants to be.

This is a phenomenon not to be feared but embraced. It's something you won't be able to spot until this point in your

On the Subject

Most of all, *I'm looking for what I meant*, because in the second draft I'll want to add scenes and incidents that reinforce that meaning.

—Stephen King

work, when you can take a step back, look at the novel as a whole, and begin to feel the "pull" of the work. What this does is offer you a framework with which to conduct your rewrite: You'll begin to see your characters in big-picture ways: getting a better, fuller sense of their personalities, which you can then bring out more consciously as you work back through the story. You'll also have a more precise sense of tone—when the mood feels right and why, when it seems incongruent with what you're attempting to do—which will help you focus your word-by-word choices in editing and rewrites. You'll even come to see your major and minor arcs in new ways. (That minor character, for example, who put you on edge whenever you brought him back into the story, though you weren't really sure why … he certainly seems rather shifty, now that you take a step back, and there's this clipped, tense tone to his voice whenever he speaks … He seems to have this anger about him, just barely held back, and he doesn't seem entirely trustworthy … so where might that be coming from, and what does this mean for his presence in the book …?)

What this process requires, first and foremost, is an ability to give your draft an almost empathic reading, paying particular attention to what feelings or vibes come up as you read it through, then figuring out what in the text evokes those particular feelings, and finally considering the implications for your story. That doesn't mean that every unexpected turn the novel or a character takes will be a correct one; there's a difference between the subconscious trying to nudge the book along and the book taking diversions of no real importance, just as there's a difference between a character trying to grow vs. one who's simply begun behaving *out* of character. You'll still have to make smart decisions, being able to recognize what's important to pursue vs. what should be minimized or gotten rid of altogether. Nevertheless, read-through and revision really are *discovery* stages, and what you discover about your work in these stages isn't going to make your job more difficult but much easier (and more exciting as you see the novel begin to take on its final shape).

IF YOU AND YOUR STORY COULD ARMWRESTLE, WHO WOULD WIN?

So what happens in those instances when your story begins leading you in directions you not only didn't anticipate but actually don't want to go? When your light-hearted story insists that, no, it's actually quite dark, or when your character who's been misbehaving finally begins rebelling outright? Who's right when you and your story are at odds? Do you let the story do what it wants? Or do you try to put your foot down and demand that it follow your directions?

This is a dilemma every writer faces at some point, and while there's no *easy* answer to the question, there's nevertheless, much to the writer's dismay, a correct one: The story is almost always right.

Trying to impose your will over a story that wants to go in a different direction almost always ends in stalemate; unless, of course, it ends the *other* way: in a bad, chaotic, disjointed ulcer-maker. So, then, your options are really three: impose your will and create the ulcer-maker, go with the story and see where it leads, or walk away.

Of these, following the story's lead seems to be the best option, the one that will cause the least immediate stress, though if you're so opposed to the direction of the story that you'd consider walking away, you might want to think about why it is you'd refuse to go along.

If it's simply a matter of ego, a matter of *you* knowing the way the story should go and settling for *nothing less* than what you see in your head, you might want to figure out why you're being so rigid, what interesting possibilities exist in other directions. Ego's a poor reason for bad writing, just as it's a poor reason for anything else, so don't forget to check it before you sit down at the keyboard. The story doesn't really belong to you; it's the other way around.

If, on the other hand, there's something about the direction of the story that fundamentally bothers you—a subject matter you find unbecoming, for instance—you might remind yourself first that writers don't write about what's easy; they write about *conflict*. Granted, not all conflicts are created equally, and some will be more interesting to you and easier to write about than others, but as a general rule conflict is something to welcome rather than avoid in your work. More than this, remember that writers don't write to show what they know but in order to question and discover what they know. Writing about difficult subject matters can require you to dig deep—and you'll occasionally hear stories of writers who are happy to finish up a novel for this very reason, because of the psychological or emotional demands of living in that headspace—but if it's done for the right reasons, in pursuit telling a compelling story, digging deep will often be worth it.

The bottom line is this: When a story has begun to take on a life of its own, it can be a futile exercise to try to wrest control away from it. Instead, follow it and see what happens, and be open to the unexpected. You might be quite pleased by the results.

REVISING THE MICRO: PROOFREADING & EDITING

Stepping back and taking a look at the emerging shape of your novel allows you to revise in the macro: rewriting, adding, or cutting scenes, sharpening characterization, bringing individual scenes in line with tone and theme, and so on. But it's important to remember that macro goals are also achieved through micro changes, through careful proofreading and targeted editing that affect the word-by-word momentum and meaning of the novel.

Proofreading and editing one's own work can be quite a task for a novelist. For one, the writer's closeness to his own work sometimes leads to quick, sloppy, and rather hopeful proofing—meaning, *I hope there aren't any mistakes*—of both language and content; it's too easy for us to begin scanning the work rather than really reading it, glossing right over any problems even when they're glaring. It can also be a challenge to hear the language of the piece as it really reads on the page, rather than how it reads in our heads—and, of course, the reader has *only* the page to go on. Finally there's the issue of fatigue; by the time we get to the proofreading stage, our eyes and minds are likely tired, having been staring at the same words for however long it's taken us to finish the draft.

On the Subject

I can't write five words but that I change seven.
—*Dorothy Parker*

Our minds, ready to turn on the tube and watch a marathon of whatever devoid-of-substance thing we can find, plays tricks on us, convinces us that everything on the page looks just fine. Now where's that remote …?

The best approach I've found to proofing and editing your own work—and one that addresses the problems above—is also pretty simple: Proofread your work out loud. Sit there and read it, exactly as it's written, to yourself. You still have to be careful that you don't fill in blanks as you read it, adding or omitting words, rearranging sentences, excusing problems; you have to read every single word, obey every punctuation mark, exactly as written. But if you do, you'll be surprised at how much you catch that you never would've seen just looking at the manuscript: repeating words or descriptions, awkward phrasings, passive language, sentences from Mars, what have you. (The out-loud approach catches more than just grammar and mechanics; substantive problems should also jump out at you.)

Another must is having a reader you trust. Sometimes this might be a family member or partner, though there should be a few grounds rules set in order to ensure it doesn't accidentally become a source of tension or provocation (even the most well-meant criticism of a work, coming from someone you love, can suddenly feel like personal rejection). First, then, you want to make sure your reader is capable of being distant and objective enough to read your work, as if a stranger had written it; that your reader is keen enough, as a reader, to articulate why he or she reacted in a certain way (there's no less helpful criticism than "I liked it" or "I didn't really like it"); and that the reader can deliver criticism in such a way that is constructive, where both of you keep in mind there's a common good and goal: making the novel the best it can be. If a family member or partner can fulfill these conditions and is willing to read your work, fantastic. If not, then you might want to look for another reader, maybe a close friend or teacher, or maybe a writing group in the area you could join. (Make sure they'd be willing to read a novel excerpt first).

Above all, remind yourself that micro-revision is what creates the macro effect. Give the process the attention it deserves.

CREATING A SYSTEM FOR YOUR PROOFREAD & EDIT

The revision stage is really about seeing your book as a whole, recognizing patterns you didn't notice before, reconciling any disparate parts into a unified whole. The best way to accomplish all of these things is to be *systematic* in your approach to revision by devising a way of clarifying what works, what doesn't, and what you need to keep an eye out for so that your goals in rewriting will be clear.

Whatever system makes sense to you is, of course, the best. Nevertheless, here are some tips that should make the process easier:

1. **Print a copy of the novel and mark it up**. Having a hard copy in front of you allows you not only to make line-by-line edits as you need but to jot down questions for later, make comments on consistency or style, find and mark (with paperclips or tabs) any scenes or moments you need to look at for comparison, and, in general, to have a conversation with the draft. You'll want your printout to be double-spaced so you have plenty of room to make comments and edits. (Also don't forget to number your pages

On the Subject

What the honest writer does, when he's finished a rough draft, is go over it and over it, time after time, refusing to let anything stay if it looks awkward, phony or forced.

—*John Gardner*

first, to help as a reference and in case your dog decides to rearrange the novel for you.)

2. Be consistent in your marks. A question mark might indeed convey the appropriate emotion when you find passages that don't make sense, or where the pacing drags, or where there's a glaring plot hole or a character who seems to act out of character. But a question mark doesn't really help you recognize one problem from the next when looking back over your notes. Be specific and consistent in your marginalia, coming up with a clear method for identifying and distinguishing types of problems you encounter. You'll of course want to keep a legend of some sort to help you keep the marks straight. Or, you might want to include these in the master document you make below.

3. Make a style guide. Publishers always create a style guide in which they make clear the stylistic, structural, and occasionally substantive needs for the project. You might want to make a master guide of your own, divided into different sections and categories to allow you to keep your notes straight: one on redundant or overused language to avoid, for example; another on timeline; another on characters and their particulars (so you don't forget that the secondary character with the fast car is named Bob Miller, not Bill Miller, as you sometimes call him); another on settings and the characters associated with them ... *anything at all* that will help you keep track of your fictional world and the line-by-line rules you've set. For examples of what such documents might look like, or what kind of information you should keep record of, see Worksheets 4: Supporting Characters, 10: Descriptions, 12: Major & Minor Settings, and 22: Subplot Tracker in the appendix and use these to help you keep your particulars straight.)

4. Keep track of problems as they occur to you. If you realize some problem or inconsistency in the novel, though it's not part of the problem you're currently working on, don't file it away in your head and promise you'll come back later; find an appropriate place on your style guide to note the problem immediately, while you still recognize and understand what the problem is.

It's important to keep a sharp mind during the proofing, editing, and rewriting stages, but it's also important to keep a good attitude. Revision isn't drudge work, punishment for having written a novel, but an opportunity to see your work in new ways and learn about it, so that the rewritten draft will be even stronger and closer to your vision for the story.

THE READ-THROUGH

When you're ready, print out a draft of your novel and begin reading through, marking anything you find, or any questions you come across, for reworking later. Keep a notebook or electronic document open for your style sheet, and look for both macro and micro problems you'll need to address later. And, again, approach your revision with gratitude for what you find rather than dread—and with a determination to make each draft of your novel better than the last.

PART THREE
COFFEE BREAK

FURTHER RESOURCES

The following is a brief list of resources that might be of help to you as you consider how to help your novel out into the world:

ON WRITING

Mystery and Manners by Flannery O'Connor
Burning Down the House: Essays by Charles Baxter
Writing Fiction by Janet Burroway
Making Shapely Fiction by Jerome Stern
Bird by Bird: Some Instructions on Writing and Life by Anne Lamott
Zen in the Art of Writing by Ray Bradbury
Plot & Structure by James Scott Bell
Gotham Writers' Workshop: Writing Fiction by Alexander Steele (Ed.)
Words Overflown by Stars by David Jauss (Ed.)

ON PUBLISHING

Writer's Market Deluxe Edition (Writer's Digest Books)
Novel & Short Story Writer's Market (Writer's Digest Books)
Guide to Literary Agents (Writer's Digest Books)
Formatting and Submitting Your Manuscript, 3rd Ed., by Chuck Sambuchino (Writer's Digest Books)
Writer's Digest (magazine)
Poets & Writers (magazine)

ONLINE RESOURCES

Publisher's Weekly online <www.publishersweekly.com>
Publisher's Lunch <www.publishersmarketplace.com/lunch/free/>
Writer's Digest online
Galley Cat <www.mediabistro.com/Galleycat/>
Poets & Writers online
AuthorLink

ORGANIZATIONS (SAMPLING)

The Association of Writers and Writing Programs, AWP <www.awpwriter.org>
Black Authors and Published Writers Directory
Society of Children's Book Writers and Illustrators <http://scbwi.org>
Science Fiction Writers Association
Mystery Writers of America
Romance Writers of America <www.rwanational.org>
(There are many other organizations out there; search for those that most appeal to you and apply to your work.)

APPENDIXES

PRACTICAL TIPS FOR THE NIGHTTIME NOVELIST

The purpose of this section is to offer some further advice on novel writing that doesn't really fit into easy categorization, though I'm hesitant to call this advice purely practical. Some of it is—you'll need a good place to work that meets your individual needs, and you should absolutely set goals and deadlines for yourself as you go—but other bits of wisdom you find here will seem more off-topic. Or superstitious. Or weird.

Of course that's fine. Take what's useful and feel free to disregard the rest. But don't forget this section is here; there might come a time when you're stuck in the work and find yourself thinking, *What the heck! I'll go take a shower.* Maybe you'll find yourself out at a dinner somewhere, about to spill the secrets of your novel writing, and will suddenly find yourself thinking, *Wait, maybe I shouldn't discuss it. I might jinx it.* Maybe you'll find yourself feeling a bit guilty for spending so much of your time locked away in a little room, separate from the world, and will need someone to tell you that your family and friends

On the Subject

I type in one place, but I write all over the house.
—*Toni Morrison*

understand that what you're doing means something to you; it's okay. Maybe you'll need some of the advice in the chapter after all, no matter how rational or irrational you find it, to help make it through as a Nighttime Novelist. And if that's the case, then who cares if any of these seem irrational? As John Lennon reminds us: Whatever gets you through the night, it's alright.

I couldn't agree more.

Here, then, presented in no particular order, are some tips that might help you get your novel written. I hope these do the trick.

And one last thing: I wish you all the best in your writing.

- **Find a workspace that meets all your needs.** Most writers require the following: privacy, quiet, access to the Internet, a bathroom, and few distractions. Figure out what you'd add to or subtract from the list, and make sure your environment meets your needs. If it doesn't, see how you can change it, or find a new workspace that'll be available any time you need it.
- **Don't check your e-mail when you work.** Or surf the Internet. Or read the news. You should have access to the Internet just in case you need to check a fact, or conduct quick research, or look for inspiration, but try to imagine the Internet has glass around it like a fire extinguisher. In case of emergency …
- **Discover your best working habits and conditions, and then make them routine.** Routine can help you access the state of mind you need, becoming more automatic (or as automatic as creativity can be). Try to stick to it.
- **When the routine stops working, change the routine.** That coffee shop really did the trick for a month, but now you're sick of it. So find a new coffee shop and make a new routine. When routine becomes rut, it's outlived its usefulness.
- **Set goals and meet them.** Some writers like achieving a daily word count—say, 1,000 words total, no matter how quickly

they come or how long they take. Others like a weekly word or page count, so if they have one bad day they can make it up the next. Find what works for you as a goal, and then meet it consistently.

- **Delegate real-world responsibilities.** If you have a family or a partner, ask them to help you take care of the practical things that need to get done: bill paying, dinner, taking out the trash, whatever. Again, if they understand your writing is important to you, they'll be happy to help. (And you can return the favor sometime if they'd like to take on some project of their own …)
- **Take care of yourself.** Don't get so wrapped up in the project that you forget to eat, sleep, recharge, and TCB. Taking care of yourself is taking care of your novel.
- **Keep a book you love nearby.** When you get stuck, or need to be inspired, open it up to a good passage and read. Let it jumpstart your creative brain.
- **Keep music you can write to.** This is different for every writer. Personally I need ambient music—no words, nothing too loud or fast-moving. Find out what kind of music you write best to and then get a lot of it. Make a playlist called "Writing Music" and keep some headphones at your desk.
- **Have some mindless activity at hand.** Sometimes getting out of your head for a few moments is the best way to solve a problem. Play solitaire for a minute. Play with a slinky. Get a little squeeze ball designed to release tension, and squeeze the life out of it.
- **Have mindless activities elsewhere.** Take a shower. Get out and take a drive or a walk. Wash the dishes. Do something that requires handiwork but no concentration.
- **Keep several kinds of YouTube videos bookmarked.** Save those that make you laugh, those that inspire you, and those that

require no thought whatsoever, for when you need to quit thinking. Use as needed (but only as needed).

- **Fill your workspace with art and objects that make you think of your story.** Choose things from the time period of your novel, or associated with your characters, or reminiscent of the book's mood, or what have you. If you work out in public, then change your laptop's wallpaper to something related.

- **Don't discuss a work in progress.** You don't need any external pressures or expectations on you when you write, not even those by well-meaning friends. If you get asked about the novel, simply say, "I'm working on something, but I'm not exactly sure what." That will confuse them long enough for you to change the subject.

- **Keep a tape recorder or journal nearby at all times.** In the car, at your bedside, in your personal bag, everywhere. As soon as you stop thinking about the novel, something will come to you. Make sure you have a way of recording it. (Don't try to scribble while driving, of course. And don't take your tape recorder into the shower.)

- **When the perfect image or idea comes to you as soon as you've gone to bed, GET OUT OF BED.** Don't tell yourself that you'll remember when you wake up. You won't.

- **Don't read while you write.** This is maybe personal preference, but I find that whatever I'm reading while working on a novel inevitably begins corrupting the novel; I start writing like whomever I'm reading. So by all means read often and read well—good writers are, obviously, good readers—but be careful about anything that might contaminate the creative process.

- **Be ritualistic and superstitious.** If you realize that your best writing days come when you've eaten chicken, then by all means: Eat chicken. Every day.

- **Cast off a bad ritual.** The moment chicken stops working for you, try pork. Or go vegetarian. Or change your socks. Or take on whatever ritual gets you going again. It doesn't matter if this is just the placebo effect. Placebos occasionally save lives.
- **Work quickly.** Especially on a first draft. Don't spend your energy fretting about what you just wrote, or what's still to come. Write with your focus on the words right now, and get them onto the page without overthinking.
- **Cut yourself some slack.** There will be days when you're the worst writer who ever lived. Everyone has those days. Tell yourself it's okay, and then keep going.
- **Write the scene that's coming to you, even if it's out of sequence.** If you're working on Act II, and suddenly an Act III scene pops into your head and comes to life, write it.
- **Don't throw anything away.** Even if that chapter or subplot isn't right for this novel, it might be right for the next. (Or, you might realize in another month that it did fit after all.) Keep versions and drafts and cut material.
- **Keep your files organized on your computer.** Make folders with versions and dates, so you'll know which draft is which. And clearly mark the draft you're currently working on so you can find it easily.
- **Celebrate milestones and victories.** Go out to dinner with your significant other, who'll be glad to see you. Buy yourself some small luxury item. Take a night off and have fun, then get right back to it the next day.
- **Don't beat yourself up over failures.** The next victory will make them all worthwhile.
- **Don't feel guilty for being so isolated and secretive.** You're doing something important, something that means a lot to you. Your loved ones and friends understand. They do.

- **Finish your writing day in the middle of a sentence.** Finishing at the end of a section or chapter can make the next day's start a slow one. Stopping in mid-sentence, as goofy as it sounds, allows you to jump right back in the next day.
- **Be prepared for false starts.** Everyone false-starts in big and small ways. It's just part of the process, but eventually it'll lead you to the right entry point into the story, or even into your day's work. Don't get discouraged by it.
- **Enjoy your work.** Enjoy your work. Enjoy your work.

WORKSHEET 1: Developing Initial Ideas

Directions: Look back to the example on page 20 of brainstorming aspects of the novel from the initial idea. Then, follow your own novel idea through the following steps and see how much of the story is already present or suggested.

Premise:

Characters:

Plot:

Tone:

Voice/POV:

Setting:

Theme:

Title:

Directions: Sketch your main character by filling in as many of the following baseline facts as you can and keeping track of any images or keywords that come to you.

Main character:

Age:

Physical description:

Internal motivation:

Internal conflict:

External motivation:

External conflict:

Potential problems with character:

WORKSHEET 3: Character & Plot Arcs

Directions: Make a sketch of your overall plot and character arcs, looking back to the examples on pages 29–31 as a guide.

WANT	WHAT STANDS IN THE WAY	RESOLUTION
External	External	External
Internal	Internal	Internal

WORKSHEET 4: Supporting Characters

Directions: Make a sketch of your supporting characters, beginning with your conception of them as you introduce them and then adding to or amending the sketches as you work through the novel.

Character name	Description/ Characteristics/ Keywords	Relevant story or backstory	Chapters/ Pages where character appears (FYI)	How character relates to/reveals protagonist

Directions: Use the graph below to sketch the basic shape of your story arc. Begin with these major moments and turning points in the overall arc, then keep this page to jot notes for scene ideas that help bridge the gaps.

ACT I		ACT II			ACT III	
Setup Inciting Incident	Plot Point 1	First Culmination	Darkest Moment	Plot Point 2	Climax	Dénouement

WORKSHEET 6: Three Lesser-Used Novel Structures

Directions: Consider the following lesser-used novel structures and consider what benefit, if any, these forms might have for your own novel.

Structure	Characteristics	Examples	Potential use for your novel
Epistolary	Most commonly told in the form of letters or diary entries, but can include grocery lists, police reports, e-mails, journals, newspaper clippings, top-ten lists, or any other kind of document that helps tell the story.	*The Color Purple* by Alice Walker *Dracula* by Bram Stoker *U.S.!* by Chris Bachelder *The Screwtape Letters* by CS Lewis	
Frame	A story within a story, or more properly, an outer story framing an inner one. Allows for a relationship and comparison between the "inside" and "outside" stories, adding up to a full experience.	*One Thousand and One Nights* *Frankenstein* by Mary Shelley *Heart of Darkness* by Joseph Conrad *The Blind Assassin* by Margaret Atwood	
Novel in Stories	A collection of linked stories featuring either the same protagonist or a cast connected in some way. Individual stories stand alone but also add up to a bigger overall arc.	*Winesburg, Ohio* by Sherwood Anderson *Love Medicine* by Louise Erdrich *Jesus' Son* by Denis Johnson *Olive Kitteridge* by Elizabeth Strout	

Directions: Look back to the section on POV and voice beginning on page 71 and then test your own narrative choices by answering the questions below.

What POV have you chosen for the novel and why? What does the selection offer you in terms of telling the story you want to tell?

Will the POV have access to all the information—external or internal—you'll need to tell the story? If not, are there ways of overcoming this, of introducing information the narrator doesn't directly know?

Will the POV be appropriate for the story in terms of its relationship to what's being said? If it's a rather personal story, for instance, is the POV close enough to convey that? If the story is emotionally complex, does the voice also have enough distance and perspective to be able to tell the story without distortion? Will it be able to strike the balance you need?

Does the POV help you find the voice, as well as the attitude conveyed? This has to do with the narrator's ability to evoke the right tone and kind of images that will convince your reader that the world of your novel exists. List any keywords—or even any full lines—that capture the mood you're looking for in the piece.

Directions: Choose one of the following first lines, take it as your own, and without planning where you're headed, write a second one that seems to fit and interests you, and then a third, and keep going. Whenever you feel satisfied enough to stop, read back over what you've written and then put it aside, let a day or so pass, then come back and choose another first line and try the exercise again. With any luck, you'll begin to see things in common from exercise to exercise: a consistent pull toward the comic or the dramatic, perhaps, or toward a particular subject matter, or a style that's more colloquial or formal, whatever. What you find in your word-by-word storytelling and its tendencies might begin to suggest your baseline voice. This exercise has worked very well with my writing students; it never ceases to amaze me how twenty writers, all starting from the same first line, can end up with twenty completely different stories, in varied styles; their own voices have begun to kick in and steer the work.

Here are the first lines to choose from. Again, don't overthink where the story should go; in fact you shouldn't look any farther than the very next line to write.

Sheila needed the money, and so against her better judgment she said yes.

In the morning I see that things have gotten worse.

Bob has that look on his face again.

I almost speak up, but at the last moment I don't say anything.

George realizes he's made a mistake two seconds too late.

Directions: For each cliché below, first determine what information or meaning is being conveyed; then conjure the event, object, or idea in your mind and re-examine it, paying particular attention to what the five senses reveal about it. Finally rewrite the line, conveying the meaning through some particular sensory detail or figurative comparison. Feel free to brainstorm, to try different things, to write down whatever comes to your head. Again, effectual description starts in exploring unconscious associations before moving into more conscious construction. (I've started the first one as an example. Please note that it's not important in the exercise to match up the POV or tense of the original line; we're just practicing our image-making here.)

Cliché	Meaning	Details	Senses	Rewritten
It's raining cats and dogs.	It's raining forcefully.	ground swampy earthworms floating up potholes burbling car tires whooshing windowpanes popping	Taste: N/A (can taste reveal the force of something?) Touch: Hard little droplets like dimes being thrown; like fat beestings Sight: Like chain mail? Like tinsel? Sound: Like fingers drumming? Like beating a pillow with your fist? Hissing? Sizzling? Smell: N/A (can smell reveal the force of something?)	Which might you turn into an effective image to convey the original's meaning? If none, what images or ideas come to mind for you?

THE NIGHTTIME NOVELIST

Cliché	Meaning	Details	Senses	Rewritten
The crowd roared.			Taste: Touch: Sight: Sound: Smell:	
She was screaming her head off.			Taste: Touch: Sight: Sound: Smell:	
The car screeched to a stop.			Taste: Touch: Sight: Sound: Smell:	
I felt my stomach drop.			Taste: Touch: Sight: Sound: Smell:	

Directions: Use the following worksheet to map out your descriptions and relevant details of the novel's major and minor settings. Look especially to how the descriptions serve not just to show the places in terms of physicality but what they mean for the protagonist and reader.

Place being described	Physical descriptors or attributes	Narrator's attitude toward the described	Feeling that should be evoked in the reader	Images/ Keywords/ Peculiar or relevant details
Major setting(s)				
Minor settings				
Objects or props				
Other ideas, objects, or motifs				

Directions: Briefly sketch those markers and pivotal moments which will determine the shape and function of the first act.

Opening Scene and Setup	Inciting Incident	Plot Point 1
introduces character and motivation	conflict which reveals personal stakes for the protagonist	turning point which changes the dynamic of the story and launches Act II

Directions: Briefly sketch your opening scene, considering above all how it introduces character and internal motivation and effectively entices the reader into the novel.

OPENING SCENE SKETCH

Summary:

Hook:

Setting:

Characters:

Arc of individual scene:

Novel arc/Question(s) introduced:

Directions: Briefly sketch Act I's Inciting Incident, the moment of external conflict that reveals the protagonist's internal stakes.

INCITING INCIDENT SKETCH

Scene summary:

How external conflict reveals the personal stakes:

Setting:

Characters:

Arc of individual scene:

Novel arc/Question(s) introduced:

Directions: Sketch each scene with an eye toward advancing the external and/or internal quest.

ACT I SCENES (establishing character and plot arcs, bridging key scenes)

Scene

Scene

Scene

Scene

Additional scenes/plot points [building toward Inciting Incident and Plot Point 1]

Directions: Sketch out Plot Point 1, the turning point that reveals external motivation or goal and leads to the story's second act.

FIRST PLOT POINT SKETCH

Scene Summary:

How external motivation or goal is introduced:

Relationship to internal motivation or goal:

Why this is a turning point (and the character can't go back or refuse):

Setting:

Characters:

Arc of scene:

Novel arc/Question(s) introduced:

Directions: Below are opening lines setting up a particular relationship and scenario. Complete the lines by choosing an adjective from the list provided and filling in the blank, and then consider what the lines suggest in terms of a scene.

My boss calls me into his office to tell me he's quitting. On his face is a look of _____.

despair	rage
hopefulness	confusion
unchecked lust	panic
recklessness	relief
accusation	guilt

Write a brief scene (250 words or so) using the above opening lines of narration as your start. Then construct a dialogue between the two characters in which this moment plays out, using the way the two speak to each other in the moment to reveal, and briefly revel in, the predicament.

Directions: Sketch each scene with an eye toward escalating conflict, building suspense, and advancing the external and/or internal quest.

ACT II SCENES
Scene

Scene

Scene

Scene

Additional scenes/plot points [building toward First Culmination and Darkest Moment]

Directions: Choose a scene from the second act to consider how you might effectively raise the stakes and tension through the following means.

Scene Summary (Include characters in the scene, arc of the scene, setting, and placement /purpose in the story)	
Conflict (What do the characters—the protagonist and others—want in the scene? Is the conflict external, internal, or both?)	External: Internal:
Tension (Does the tension in the scene come between the protagonist and someone or something else? Is the tension public or professional? Personal and private? What's at stake in the scene?)	
Building Suspense (What opportunities exist to build tension by turning down the volume in narration or dialogue? How might going quiet make the tension more palpable?)	
Pacing (How might you draw out the tension while keeping the focus and pacing of the scene tight? What tricks of time and place or subjective focus can you use?	

WORKSHEET 21: Deepening the Protagonist

Directions: As your protagonist faces escalating conflicts in the second act, consider how your understanding of the character, and the character's complexity, has grown by answering the following questions.

What aspect of the character's personality is her biggest asset?

What aspect of the character's personality might be her undoing?

What is the character most afraid of?

What are her weaknesses, whether mental, emotional, physical, or psychological?

What are her strengths, whether mental, emotional, physical, or psychological?

What will have to change about the character, or what will she have to overcome in her own nature, in order to be successful in her quest?

What in the character's past is reflected in the current motivation and/or conflict?

Directions: Use the following worksheet to consider the function of your novel's subplots and how to keep them advancing the main plot and character arcs.

Subplot and character(s) involved	Motivations of protagonist and secondary character(s) in subplot	How subplot helps reveal protagonist and larger story/character arcs	How (and when) the subplot should resolve	Chapters/ pages where subplot comes in

WORKSHEET 23: First Culmination & Darkest Moment

Directions: Sketch these Act II moments where the protagonist nears the goal and fails, or suffers a loss or setback.

FIRST CULMINATION/DARKEST MOMENT SKETCH

Scene summary:

What protagonist is within reach of in the scene:

What the loss means for the external or internal quest:

Setting:

Characters:

Arc of individual scene:

Novel arc/Question(s) introduced:

Directions: Sketch the turning point where protagonist makes one last push toward the goal, leading to Act III.

PLOT POINT 2 SKETCH

Scene summary:

Given the loss at the Darkest Moment, describe what convinces the protagonist to make one last push.

Are the stakes at this turning point clear? Is it clear what he hopes to gain in Act III by facing the conflict directly?

Is the original internal motivation—as well as the external—still present and recognizable in the story?

Setting:

Characters:

Arc of individual scene:

Novel arc/Question(s) introduced:

Directions: Briefly sketch your novel's final act.

Climax / Final Culmination	Dénouement	Result
moment of direct conflict for the character, with everything he's hoped for at stake	the winding down that reveals how the story has come full circle	what the character and reader are left with
		External motivation or goal met: Internal motivation or goal met:

Directions: Consider your novel's Climax, the point where the protagonist faces the conflict directly, with his external quest or goal on the line.

CLIMAX SKETCH

Scene summary:

How is the protagonist's external motivation or goal at risk in the scene?

What does he hope to accomplish if he succeeds?

Does the protagonist succeed or fail at this moment?

Setting:

Characters:

Arc of individual scene:

Has the external arc or quest been tied up by the end?

WORKSHEET 27: Dénouement & Closing Scenes

Directions: Consider the novel's post-climax scenes with an eye toward tying up unresolved arcs and the novel as a whole.

DÉNOUEMENT SKETCH

Scene summary:

How the Dénouement recalls the opening of the book and the overall internal motivation:

Tone that should be struck at the end of the book ... the feeling the reader should take away with him:

Setting:

Characters:

Arc of individual scene:

Have all outstanding minor subplots or arcs been successfully tied up?

What resonant moment or image should the novel end on?

INDEX